T0274163

DANISH
FOLK TALES

SVEND-ERIK ENGH

ILLUSTRATED BY TEA BENDIX

First published 2023

The History Press
97 St George's Place, Cheltenham,
Gloucestershire, GL50 3QB
www.thehistorypress.co.uk

British Library Cataloguing in Publication Data.
A catalogue record for this book is available from the British Library.

ISBN 978 1 80399 366 9

Typesetting and origination by The History Press
Printed and bound in Great Britain by TJ Books Limited, Padstow, Cornwall.

Trees for LYfe

CONTENTS

FOREWORD

Let me introduce you to Svend-Erik Engh, one of my favourite storytellers. First of all he is a very, very tall man, slim-built and pretty bald. Everything about him seems quite smoothed out till you see the expressive mobility of his face, which is often wreathed in smiles, or open-mouthed in interest and astonishment at what you are telling him. That is Svend-Erik the person, and Svend-Erik Engh the storyteller.

About forty years ago I saw Dario Fo, the Italian storyteller and theatre maker, perform live at the Edinburgh Festival. He came on stage with a scruffy cardigan hanging round his very tall and lean body. He began talking to us in a low key, natural manner. Then gradually his tale of mediaeval priests and rogues took shape, and his body and face began to move with the story. Soon every part of Dario was willowing and weaving, wobbling and occasionally jerking, all to express action, characters and emotions. Yet there was still control remaining at the centre, a cunning identification with the tale that simultaneously used every means at the storyteller's disposal to share its development.

Svend-Erik is in the great European tradition of Dario Fo's artistry. He begins in a natural low-key mode till he establishes a genial rapport with his listeners and then he uses his gifts of expression to usher us into the story experience. Moving face and increasingly form, Svend-Erik draws us through the tale with a full gamut of emotions, liberal doses of humour and an under-girding of humane understanding.

This approach to storytelling is firmly rooted in Svend-Erik Engh's Scandinavian culture, in particular its educational traditions, as inspired by N.F.S. Grundtvig, the great Danish philosopher of poetry and myth. Here is Svend-Erik's own account of falling into the art of storytelling:

> The first story I told was to my students when I was a Folkhøjskole teacher in 1993. It was at a morning assembly and every morning the teacher was supposed to give them a personal message, it could be a film, a book, something from the news, something that that teacher thought could interest the students coming to the school in the morning. It was my debut as a storyteller. It went well. They listened in another way from when I had chosen to read out loud from a book. And when we had lunch together that day I heard my story being retold to some of the students that missed out the morning assembly. No students had ever done that with any of my readings or if I had shown them a film. I was hooked on this thing called storytelling. And since that morning I have told stories in schools, in working places, to people in a park in Copenhagen and, after I moved to Edinburgh, often at the Scottish Storytelling Centre.

Human engagement and communication: here lies the origin and the purpose of Svend-Erik's art. Yet his grassroots storytelling has been combined with a distinguished contribution to education of all kinds through storytelling. He is an excellent course and workshop leader, who has never lost the teaching gift, or his keen interest in Grundtvig's philosophy of education.

We are delighted to have Svend-Erik Engh living and working in Scotland, though also pleased to share him with the rest of Britain, with his Danish homeland and with Norway and Sweden, to which he has close ties. Scotland has an integral Norse dimension to its culture and stories, and Svend-Erik's presence reminds us that we are part of a community of northern nations.

Now in this fine collection of stories, Svend-Erik Engh has dug into his own Danish heritage and art to celebrate its contribution to world storytelling. He explains his approach to making this collection as follows:

> This book contains fairy tales and legends, and the term folk tales brings together both of these kinds of stories. As a storyteller, I tell the stories I love. *Danish Folk Tales* is a collection of my favourite stories.

One of the first fairy tales I told was The Sevenstar, one of the stories in this collection. I had told this story many times to my then three-year-old daughter. And one evening in December we were just home from a trip to the library and the stars were twinkling in the black sky. My daughter looked up at them even before she was completely out of the car and asked me eagerly 'Where's the Sevenstar, Daddy?' I stopped, turned around, looked up, and was blinded by a street lamp. So I told her to walk with me into the darkness. My daughter held my hand tightly as we moved away from the street light, and together we looked up into the twinkling night sky. We were silent for a moment. It felt good to be alive. 'There it is!' I said pointing upward. 'Which one of them is the princess?' said my daughter. And there we stood choosing which star was which character in the story.

I would love it if you tell these stories out in the world and see what truths they reveal for people. Allow these stories to feed your reality.

The first legend I told was from stories I had found about Caroline Mathilde, the English princess who came to Denmark in 1766 to marry Christian VII, a mad king. She had a serious affair with Johan Struensee from Altona near Hamburg, then a part of Denmark. I lived close to a restaurant called Jægerhytten, the Hunting Cottage, where the two lovers were supposed to have had some of their romantic meetings. The restaurant invited me to tell the legends about their love to their guests. I needed to find some surprising element of the story especially, after the release of a blockbuster film about their love. I found a drawing on the wall of the restaurant of the queen and her lover riding along the coast of Denmark and she was sitting as queens were supposed to, side saddle. But that was not how Caroline rode her horse. I had found many descriptions of how offended people were because Caroline would in fact straddle her horse like a man. Her days in this forest with her lover were a time of freedom, and liberation for the queen. A time when she could be herself.

It is a little different to tell legends from fairy tales. You have to know the history and then you can build your story, create clear images and make the characters real people. And a little unexpected surprise always helps.

It is an honour and a pleasure to introduce new readers and listeners to this outstanding collection of Danish folk tales. But it is an even greater delight to introduce you to Svend-Erik the storyteller. Enjoy!

Donald Smith
Director of Scottish International Storytelling Festival

INTRODUCTION

My hope for these stories in this book is that you will tell them in your way and so they will change and become your stories as I have made them mine.

The book you are sitting with is my interpretation of each story and then with the help of storyteller, native English speaker and my life partner Alice Fernbank it has been translated from my twisted Danish mind to understandable English.

When I look at the stories collected in this book, I can hear the storytellers tell some of the people collecting these stories more than hundred years ago. I feel happy when I, among all the voices of old people, hear a schoolboy named Anders Gregersen, from Sjørslev, Jutland, who has told the story 'The Devil and the Blacksmith' to Evald Tang Kristensen. Who was this schoolboy? Where did he hear the story? Telling stories from mouth to heart was a natural part of human life in the days of Anders. It was people's way of creating some sense in a harsh reality.

So thank you Evald Tang Kristensen, one of the world's most persistent collectors of stories. You always mentioned from whom you had heard the story when you wrote the story down and published it. The number of stories you have collected is overwhelming and I admire the way that you did it, living in poor conditions with the storytellers and really trying to write down the stories exactly as they were told to you. And you stayed with the storytellers long enough, so they told you everything, including the stories that were full of troubled images or full of words that the people from the nice families didn't like. In that way you are very different from any of the collectors of stories that are famous now for collecting folk tales: Grimm in Germany, Asbjørnsen and Moe in Norway and in Denmark Svend Gruntvig. You are definitely very different from Hans Christian Andersen, who always puts himself in front of the story and makes sure that nobody can be offended.

So use the stories in this book to be inspired, maybe to visit some of the places I describe. Use the book to be troubled by some of the images and then always remember that the stories were meant to be told and that was a common experience between the storyteller and the listener, so the storyteller could adjust the stories in that moment to the listener's response to the story. 'The Princess who Became a Man' is the story in this collection with the most troublesome images, so when you read it be with somebody that you trust and if the image feels too strong, talk about it, find a way to make it a useful experience for you. And you could, of course, just skip that story and read 'The Fat Cat', a lovely little joke – I hope I don't offend anyone by using the word 'fat' about a cat – stories are like that, some are deep and troublesome, some are just plain funny and there are no bigger ideas behind them.

And do yourself a favour and scroll through the illustrations of Tea Bendix, then if you have found something intriguing that has caught your eye, take a deeper look at the drawings. Each of these illustrations has told me a new story. Tea has found a new dimension in the relations between the characters and the landscapes in the stories – just notice the ant in the tree in 'The Shoemaker's Boy'. She has spotted something deeper than I have with my simple twisted Danish mind. To work with Tea has been such a joy.

My former father-in-law, Hans Christian Rasmussen, is another story collector and totally unknown for being that. He heard the stories you will find as the last four stories in the book when he was a child in Lolland in the southern part of Denmark. He heard them from Axel Paaske, one of his uncles I think. And I was lucky enough to be part of his family for many years and he was inspired to write these stories down and gave them to me. So you will find these four stories are unique to this collection. Thanks to my former wife, Connie Bloch, for letting me include them in this book.

And thanks to my three children for being who you are, tall and wonderful. I remember every story I told you and it makes me smile and inspires me to tell more.

Alice Fernbank, my fellow storyteller and life partner.
You made it possible for me to write this book in a language
I have not mastered like you. You brought clarity to each
of the stories as the master storyteller you are.

Yours faithfully, Svend

1

DANMARK

Why Danmark is called Danmark.

Once there was a young prince and he had nothing to do. He was the youngest of three brothers. The oldest, Øster, was going to be king of Uppsala when their father died. The second, Nor, was going to be king of the land we now call Norway. But the youngest had not been granted any land to rule.

The prince wanted to make his mark in the world, to be someone, to be recognised. The land to the south was dangerous, it was a belt of forest not yet ruled by men of honour, but by wild beasts and robbers. So the young prince went to his father, King Ypper of Uppsala, and asked for men and ships, which he was granted.

One beautiful spring day with the cliffs shining in the sun they headed south across the Baltic Sea and past a rocky island we know today as Bornholm. Then they sailed towards the north and entered a narrow sea channel between two lands. Both sides of that channel were covered in lush green forests and fields, and all along both coastlines were small clusters of mud huts. The waters were crowded with fishing boats and men hauled nets full of herring ashore. Women filled baskets with fish and carried them to their homes. The prince's men flung their nets out into the water and within moments the nets were full of silvery herring.

This green land was inviting for the young prince, he knew he could be king here.

They followed the coastline until they came to a deep narrow fjord. They journeyed across the waters of the fjord until their ships arrived at the mouth of a river. On foot they followed the small river upstream until they came to a hill. The prince climbed that hill and looked at the landscape. He saw fresh water bubbling from a spring, and the green hilly landscape ready to cultivate and create fields for the future gathering of huts. The small lakes were filled with fish and the fjord wasn't far away with lots of herring. Green forests were filled with game.

The prince knew he could rule here. He had his men build a king's hall, and so he became the first king of Lejre.

One day two men dressed as soldiers asked for permission to speak to the King of Lejre. The men wore armour and had a spear in one hand and a shield in the other. Still, it was clear to the soldiers from the north that these two men were no soldiers, they were farmers dressed in warrior clothes. They were told to leave their weapons and armour outside the king's hall and when they entered the great hall the new king said hello to the two peasants.

'We are told that you are a mighty warrior king,' said the tallest of the two men. 'We think you are the only one to help us. The Saxons in the south are gathering a great army and if we should fight them alone, it will be the end of an independent Jutland, it will just be a province in the mighty Saxon empire.'

'Is there anything you have done to prevent the Saxons from coming into your land?' said the king.

'We have built a wall,' said the tall man. 'We call it Kovirke. It stretches from the west and nearly all the way over to the eastern coastline. Kovirke is on the border between Jutland in the north and the Saxons in the south, but we are not sure if it is strong enough to hold back the Saxon army.'

'What can you offer in return if I help you?' said the king.

'We can't offer much,' said the tall man. 'We are mostly farmers and fishermen and our little army is not going to be any match for the Saxons and the Saxon emperor Augustus will then rule over Jutland. If we lose he will come after you.'

'Good,' said the king. 'We will sail out towards the south of Jutland tomorrow. And you will join us and show us the way.'

Dan gathered his warriors who were happy to have something real to do instead of farming, and followed the two men to Kovirke in the southern part of Jutland. When Dan and his warriors joined the battle, the Jutes advanced against the emperor of the Saxons. The Saxons were crushed in the battle with many men lost, so many that Jutland did not have to fear another invasion from the south for many years.

After the war, the men of Jutland held a ting. They invited the men of the Island Funen to attend and told them of the hero king who had defended their country. The decision was unanimous; they all wanted the King of Lejre to be crowned King of Jutland and Funen too.

So the new King of Lejre had made his mark. He was now king over a kingdom that stretched from Skagen (Scaw) in the north to Kovirke in the south and from the long coastline of Vesterhavet (North Sea) in the west to the shore of the Baltic Sea in Skåne (Scania) to the east.

When the new king was crowned, he stood on the magic stone.

The men all cheered and called out in celebration of the new king: 'Hail, King Dan! Hail, King Dan!'

King Dan said to the men gathered from around his kingdom, 'This land is fair and fertile, the waters are filled with fish and the people are strong men and women working hard. Yet, it has one flaw – it lacks a name.'

They answered him, 'You are Dan, and therefore the land shall be called Danmark.'

The Danish word 'mark' means 'field' – 'Danmark' is 'Dan's Field'.

2

KING SKJOLD

If you spotted a Viking ship it meant trouble.

It was early morning. The fishermen were getting ready to sail out into the middle of the narrow fjord where their nets would be filled with herring and eels. The farmers came out of their small mud huts to look after their livestock or go to the fields. It was late spring and the blackbirds were busy telling everyone who wanted to listen that another lovely day had begun. Then in a split second everyone froze as a loud cry from the north end of the fjord called 'Vikings!' and fear shot into the hearts of every single human being all the way down and up Roskilde Fjord. Time stood still and even the blackbirds understood that something bad was going to happen and stopped their singing.

It was a slow-moving Viking ship that had been spotted on its way into the fjord and now farmers and fishermen on both sides of the fjord rushed to the fire stands and started the warning fires. The ship was a typical Viking warrior ship with a dragon in front and a square sail on its mast.

On both sides were round shields covered with brown calf-skin, showing that the men aboard that ship were ready to fight anyone coming near it.

There was nearly no wind and the ship sailed slowly towards the southern end of the fjord. No oarsmen were to be seen on the ship and the silence was unbearable for the farmers and fishermen waiting for the wild horde of Vikings to jump down from the ship and kill, rape and loot.

The women and children and the old folks were trying to run away from the village as fast as they could, which wasn't fast at all. The last woman to flee was the potter's wife and she turned around to get a final glimpse of her husband.

It was a miserable sight to see the men with their rakes and wooden clubs, a few spears and one or two shields waiting for the roaring Vikings. The men held their makeshift weapons, getting ready to at least hold back the intruders long enough for the villagers to escape. The potter's wife caught the eyes of her beloved husband, who smiled bravely at her. He saw their newborn tied to her back and he felt that overwhelming love for his family that always made him breathless. Then they all heard the sound of the ship landing on the banks of sand. The men bowed their heads ready to die. But nothing happened.

The potter's wife, instead of running away to safety, slowly approached the fjord. Then they all heard it. A baby crying. First the potter thought it was the baby on his wife's back, but when he looked at her, she shook her head and pointed at the ship. He raised himself from his hiding place in the dunes and looked bewildered as he saw his wife walking out into the water towards the side of the ship.

The potter's wife climbed aboard and in the middle of the ship she found a baby lying on a shield covered with sheepskin. She took the baby, unleashed her blouse and fed it right there. When the potter climbed aboard he saw his wife with their baby happily sleeping on her back and a stranger baby boy suckling at her breast as though he had never done anything else in his life. She pointed at the shield in the middle of the ship where she had found the boy. Around it was so much gold and silver that it made the potter speechless.

'You had better tell the others,' she said.

The potter stood up and shouted, 'There are no Vikings here. There's just a baby boy!'

All the men laughed with relief. The women and the old folks and the children came out from their hiding places and the celebration lasted all day and long into the night.

It was decided that the potter and his wife should raise the boy. And so they did. He was the strongest, cleverest and most gentle boy you could imagine. He loved his family, even though he knew they were not his blood. They called him Skjold, the Danish word for shield.

One day when he was only fifteen, a bear attacked him. Skjold killed the bear with his bare hands.

The rumour of a strong young man, born as a prince with gold and silver to prove it, spread and came to Lejre, where there was a need for a king. Skjold left the village by the fjord, said goodbye to his family and became King Skjold in Lejre, who ruled all the land. When people spoke of King Skjold they said that he was the son of Odin and was destined to rule the Danes. King Skjold did rule wisely for many years and with the Saxon Queen Alvilda he had many sons and daughters. The children of Skjold and Alvilda were called Skjoldunger and from them lots of stories came of bravery, wisdom and kindness.

And if women were part of a Viking army they called them Skjoldmøer in respect to the old King Skjold.

When King Skjold died, they brought him back to the ship he came on. They gave him a shield covered with sheepskin to rest his head upon and gave him silver and gold for his journey. Then they launched the Viking ship out into Roskilde Fjord like the ship had entered the fjord many years before.

3

TORA AND RAGNAR

'Lind' means soft or bendy; 'orm' is the Swedish word for a snake.

Where the River Göta met the sea the land was called Götaland. There three kingdoms met: Denmark from the south, Norway from the north and Sweden from the east.

In that land a jarl (a Scandinavian word for a king of a small piece of land) had a daughter named Tora whom he loved more than anything in the world. He had built a house for her and every day he brought her a gift. One day he gave her a tiny lindorm: a slim, green, snake lying sweetly in a little box. The snake was lying on gold coins and as it grew so did the number of gold coins beneath it.

Time passed and Tora grew into a beautiful young woman and was ready to be wedded to a suitable man. But as she had grown, so had the slithering, green snake and it was too big to live indoors so it lay outside and wrapped itself around the entire house. It was as thick as a barrel of mead and under it lay a treasure of gold coins. But the snake who had once been her beloved pet had now become her fierce protector and would not allow any man to come close.

One day a young man from the village tried. He approached the house determined to rescue the beautiful Tora. He raised his sword and charged at the snake, which lifted its head and spat poisonous venom over the young man's body. He died instantly. Tora watched from inside feeling angry and helpless.

No man from the region ever tried to rescue Tora after that.

Tora's father was desperate to free her. He announced to all three kingdoms that any man brave enough to overcome the lindorm and release his daughter would be granted the lovely Tora and all the gold lying beneath the snake.

Across the sea in Denmark there was a young Viking warrior called Ragnar who was preparing a voyage to Greenland with his men, when he heard about the beautiful young woman who was imprisoned by a lindorm. He and his men boarded their ship in high spirits equipped with food, weapons and fur-lined clothing for the cold winds of the north.

Before leaving Denmark, Ragnar had taken his hooded fur-lined coat and trousers and turned them inside out. He had then dipped the coat and trousers in tar and hidden them from his men.

On their way to Greenland they sailed along the west coast of Scandia and Halland. As they passed Götaland, Ragnar told his men to stop and get supplies on land. They anchored in a bay not far from Tora's house.

Next morning before his men woke up, Ragnar put on his tar-covered trousers and coat. On the beach he rolled in the sand, making sure that it stuck to the tar on his clothes to create a protective coating from the snake's venomous spit. He then took his spear and loosened its head from the shaft, so it would be easy to pull the shaft away.

Silently he crept towards the back entrance of Tora's house. The snake was busy watching for intruders at the front door, so it didn't discover Ragnar before he shouted, 'I am here, you monster!' and stabbed the middle of the lindorm with his spear several times, knowing that it would bounce back off its thick scaly skin. Tora, hearing the deep voice of Ragnar from the back of the house, ran to her kitchen window and couldn't believe what she saw, a strange-looking creature covered in sand tormenting the snake with his spear.

The lindorm swiftly slithered round the house to the back door and spat its venom over Ragnar, expecting to see him shrivel and die. But Ragnar's hairy breeches and his coat covered in tar and sand protected him from the poison. He aimed his spear and threw it swiftly into the soft skin below the snake's throat, piercing its heart. The lindorm gave a final hiss and its head crashed to the ground. Tora felt the whole house shaking as the snake collapsed.

Ragnar then pulled the shaft from the head of the spear and looked up. There she was, looking at him from the kitchen window. She was stunningly beautiful. He turned and walked down the hill towards his ship and his men.

When his men saw him coming, all covered in tar and sand they laughed. They gathered on the beach and Ragnar told them about his adventure.

'What happened to the gold?' said one.

'And the girl, where is she?' said another.

'They will come, I am sure. We just have to wait here,' said Ragnar.

Tora stepped out from her house to see that the snake was indeed dead. Her father came running up the hill to the house.

'The lindorm is dead,' Tora said.

She found the head of Ragnar's spear in the heart of the snake and pulled it out.

'What happened?' her father said, 'Who killed the lindorm?'

'I don't know,' Tora said, 'it was like a black bear covered in sand and when it saw me, it ran down the hill.'

'We must find out who did this and give him his reward,' said the Jarl. 'Whoever's shaft fits this spearhead is the one.'

The next day young men from across the region came to the jarl's hall carrying spear shafts in the hope that theirs would fit the head of the spear, but none did. Outside the hall Tora stood waiting for her father to call her in when they had found the one who had killed the lindorm. As she stood there she noticed the Viking ship lying out in the bay. The Vikings had not been invited and as Tora thought about it, her saviour could easily have been one of them, something that her father wouldn't approve of.

By and by her father came out of the hall shaking his head. None of the men's shafts fitted the head.

'It could be one of the Vikings,' Tora said, 'you know they have been lying in the bay for three days now.'

Her father looked bewildered at his daughter. She didn't look frightened by the prospect that it could be a Viking that had saved her and therefore deserved to be married to her.

Reluctantly he walked down towards the Viking ship and Tora followed her father down to the shore.

The jarl called out to the men on the ship, holding up the head of the spear, 'Good day, brave men, is there anyone on your ship that has a spear that could fit to this head?'

The men gathered together on the ship and looked. One of them said that it could be Ragnar's. 'Oh, yes,' said another in a casual manner like it didn't mean anything, 'we can ask him.'

And the Vikings laughed out loud as if something was really funny that the jarl couldn't see. He was about to ask what was so funny, when the men stepped aside to let Ragnar come forward. Tora gasped. She had expected a black hairy monster, but what she saw made her heart quicken. Ragnar was a handsome, strong young warrior king and when he spoke it was a real man speaking.

'What do you want?' he said in this deep dark voice that Tora felt she already knew so well even though she had just heard it twice by now.

'I want to find the man who killed the lindorm,' said the jarl, 'so I can give him his gold.'

'There was another prize,' said Ragnar, 'can I see her?'

The jarl stepped aside and Ragnar saw the young woman again. A moment passed, but it was like an eternity for Tora. Then the handsome Viking king jumped into the water and walked towards her. He had the shaft of a spear in his hand, and when he came on the beach, he gave the shaft to the jarl. It fitted the head perfectly. Tora smiled and looked into Ragnar's eyes. She took his hand and the men on the ship let out a cheer. The gold was brought down to the ship and that night the mead flowed and the Vikings celebrated their new fortune and their new queen.

Tora followed the Vikings all the way to Greenland and when winter came she followed them back to Denmark. Every day she enjoyed her freedom, a freedom given to her by her husband, Ragnar.

4

KRAKA AND RAGNAR LODBROG

In English he is known as Ragnar Lothbrok. The Danish word lodden means hairy. Ragnar Lodbrog means Ragnar hairy breeches.

After the liberation of Tora, Ragnar was known far and wide as Ragnar Lodbrog, and the couple had many sons and daughters.

But the happy days didn't last forever. Tora died and Ragnar couldn't stand being in their home with all the memories, so he gave the crown to the eldest of their sons and went on another Viking crusade.

This story tells how Ragnar met Kraka.

Aslaug was raised by her mother's father, Helmer. When in his care her parents were killed in conflicts over love and Helmer was certain that Aslaug was in danger too. Fearing for her life, he made a harp and hid the little girl inside it together with much gold and silver.

He covered his face in dirt and dressed in old clothes so he looked like a beggar. With the harp on his back he walked from village to village begging for food and playing his harp.

When they were alone, he let Aslaug out from her hiding place and she often danced by the small rivers in the night without anyone seeing her. That way they travelled from Denmark in the south to what we now call Norway in the north.

Helmer had travelled far and he was tired and hungry. He saw some lights and he found his way into a rundown farm, where he knocked on the door. An old woman opened it and looked out with an angry grunt.

The old woman, Grima, was wretched and ugly, and so dirty that she stank.

She looked at the beggar and his harp and asked harshly, 'What do you want?'

'I want a place to stay for the night,' the beggar told her, 'some warmth for my cold limbs and a bit of bread to fill my stomach.'

'You can't have that here,' she said. 'We don't have any of the things you are talking about.'

Grima wanted to close the door, but the beggar forced his way into the house, saying that he was not in the mood for a long conversation. And that the woman should give a wanderer what he asked for.

'Your farm is the only farm for many miles and I am not willing to walk any more today,' he said. 'Travellers are normally welcomed into people's homes with food and a place to sleep. Please start the fire, I got cold out in the harsh wind.'

Grima started the fire.

'There is some dark bread over there, please give me some,' the beggar said. She grunted and threw the bread at him.

While he was eating, Grima took a better look at the beggar and suddenly she frowned. Under his dirty black shirt she saw a bracelet of gold. And when she examined the harp she noticed a thread of silver. And suddenly she was very friendly towards the stranger.

'You can of course sleep here if you want,' Grima said, 'but I am sorry it is not good for you to sleep inside our house. You see, me and my husband always argue the whole night, we wouldn't let you have a quiet moment. But the barn is full of soft hay to lie on.'

Helmer took his harp and went to sleep in the barn.

When Grima's husband, Åge, came home from work in the forest, Grima told him that they could get rich if they just killed the man sleeping in the barn. Åge didn't like it, but Grima was persistent, and in the middle of the night Åge went into the barn with an axe and killed Helmer.

They took the bracelet off his arm and the harp was brought into their house. They split the wood of the harp with the axe to see what was inside and when Åge saw it was another mouth to feed, he was furious. But Grima was delighted with all the silver and gold.

'What are we going to do to that little girl?' Åge said.

'We can just tell people that it is my child,' said Grima.

'Look at yourself and look at the girl with her golden hair and soft white skin, she is the daughter of a king, that is clear,' Åge said.

Grima cut the hair of the little girl, covered her face in soot and called her Kraka, which is the Danish word for crow. She gave a black hood to the little girl and told her never to take it off and never to say a word.

Kraka grew up on the farm black as a crow, covered in dirt working day and night for Grima. Whenever somebody asked, Grima told them that the girl was her daughter and she was dumb and couldn't speak.

Many years went by, and one day Ragnar and his men sailed past the southern tip of Norway and the Vikings decided to anchor and let two of the men go ashore. They were to ask on the farm if they could use the oven to make some bread. They had flour with them from Denmark and it was the only place they could make the dough and bake the bread for miles around. Kraka was milking the goats when the two men came ashore. She looked out to sea and saw Ragnar standing on the ship. She left the goats and went to the river, where she washed her hair and her face for the first time in years.

When asked if they could bake bread, Grima just said that she couldn't stop them from doing it and that her dumb daughter would help them.

Kraka appeared and the two Vikings with the bread couldn't take their eyes off her. She started the fire and helped them make the dough, and placed the bread in the hot oven. As it was baking the two Vikings forgot all about the bread as Kraka just stood in the kitchen smiling at them. They only remembered when the kitchen filled with smoke from the oven.

When Ragnar saw the black burned bread he asked his two trusted Vikings what had happened. When the two men described Kraka and told Ragnar how beautiful the woman was, with her long golden hair going all the way down to her hips, he asked, 'Is this woman even more beautiful than my Tora?'

The men nodded silently.

'I must see this wonderful woman,' Ragnar said. 'Go and invite her to come here tomorrow morning, so I can see if you are right. But tell this Kraka that she should arrive here neither dressed nor undressed, neither fasting nor eating and neither alone nor in company.'

When Kraka received the invitation Grima stood in the doorway listening to the two Vikings. When they had returned to the ship, Grima said that this Viking must be out of his mind. 'No one can do what he asks of you,' she said. 'Forget about him and do your work.'

But Kraka knew that Ragnar was testing her.

Next morning she went to Åge and borrowed a fishing net that she wore like a dress. She found an onion and took one bite of the onion. She called for the dog on the farm to follow her.

When Ragnar saw the woman coming down towards the Viking ship wearing a fishing net, saw her bite the onion and noticed her companion, he knew that this woman was something special. Not only was she, as described by his men, stunningly beautiful, but she was also wise.

He asked her to follow him on their crusade. And for the first time since childhood she opened her mouth and spoke. 'No,' she said, 'I will be here with my foster parents. I will wait for you and if you still want me when you return in the autumn, I will follow you to Denmark.'

Then Ragnar wanted to give her a golden dress.

'Thank you,' she said, 'but I have to refuse your gift till you come back. It wouldn't work for me to have a golden dress when I live and work together with Grima and Åge on this filthy farm. If you only want me dressed in gold, forget about me. I am black Kraka taking care of the goats and making sure the fire is burning in the house.'

Ragnar said that he most certainly would return.

And he did. Autumn came with a Viking ship, and Kraka went to her foster parents and told them she was leaving. She told them that she knew that they had killed Helmer and although she had endured beatings and had been forced into hard labour, she would not punish them for any of their crimes.

She went down to the ship and followed Ragnar to Denmark, where they lived together for many years.

5

KING LINDORM

A Lindorm is a slithering, green snake filled with venom and to conquer it you need an old woman's wisdom.

Once upon a time there was a king and a queen who loved each other dearly. But there were never any children from the love, deep and warm as it was. It was of deep concern, mostly for the queen as the king could always start a war and therefore have his mind occupied elsewhere.

One day the queen went for a walk and she found a lovely peaceful clearing in the middle of the forest. She sat down on a tree trunk and started crying softly. Suddenly the queen heard a voice. 'I know what troubles you and I can help you,' said an old woman standing in front of her.

The queen looked at the old woman and her ragged dress. 'There is nothing you can do,' said the queen, 'it is a matter between me and the king.'

'You are sad because you haven't given an heir to the king,' said the old woman. 'Believe it or not, but I can help you with that.'

'I'm sorry, but I don't believe you,' said the queen. 'Nobody can help me!'

The old woman said: 'Listen to me well what you have to do to get a child. You shall take your mug, the one with big ears so you can lift it from the grass in the morning. Then place the mug tonight upside down in the north-western corner of your garden. Tomorrow morning when you lift the mug, you will find two roses. One is red and one is white. Now you have to make a choice. You shall eat one of them, only one of them. If you eat the red rose, the child that you are going to have will be a boy. If you eat the white rose, the child will be a girl. I wish you good luck with everything.'

The old woman turned around and left the queen sitting on the trunk, in deep thought. She did not know what to think. She wasn't sure if she believed in the magic power of the old woman, but on the other hand she had nothing to lose.

In the evening the queen found her mug and went into the garden and placed it in the north-western corner. And then she went up to get some sleep.

The first thing she did the next morning was to go down to the mug. She lifted it and found that the old woman had spoken the truth, at least about the roses. There were two roses under the mug, a red rose and a white rose. She sat down and tried to imagine the life of a boy.

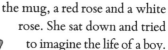

He would eventually leave her and die in a war. And if the child was going to be a girl, she would just leave her to get married somewhere far away from her. And suddenly she couldn't clearly remember how it was. If she ate the red rose would the child become a boy or was it the opposite? The queen got herself whirled into a series of thoughts and in the end she couldn't hold them out to one and another. She ate the red rose and it tasted so good that she ate the white rose as well. She thought that no harm was done and that she could have twins.

Soon after everybody could see that the queen was pregnant and the king was the happiest man in the world. The queen never told the king about the old woman and the roses. She wasn't sure that her husband would approve of having an old woman, a witch, helping her make the baby when they couldn't themselves.

Finally the days of waiting were over. The queen lay in her bed in labour. The kingdom's best midwife was there to assist the queen in the delivery. She told the queen that there was probably more than one child. So the queen thought that it would be twins and it would be both a girl and a boy, one for the red rose and one for the white rose. The midwife shrieked when the first born left the womb of the queen. It was a little green snake that slithered down on the floor and disappeared into one tiny crack in the floor. The queen didn't see clearly what it was, so the midwife whispered into her ear that she had just given birth to a green snake. The queen immediately forbade the midwife to tell the king. Then the queen felt the pressure of the second child. And when she had given birth to that child, the midwife triumphantly lifted a little baby boy up into the arms of the queen. When the king came into the room the happiness of the little family was complete. He looked at the little boy and loved him as only a father can love his son.

The boy grew up to become a clever and handsome prince, so when it was time his father told him to ride out in the kingdom to search for a suitable princess to marry. He would have to go to a neighbouring kingdom to find a daughter to wed. The prince saddled his favourite horse, bid his parents farewell and rode off.

As he came riding on the road headed south, he came to a crossroad. On the crossroad there was a strange green creature lying in the middle of the road. As the prince came closer he saw it was the biggest green snake he had ever seen, a lindorm. There was no way the prince could pass the snake lying there blocking the road. The lindorm was as thick as a man's thighs and it slithered and wriggled when the prince came closer. It lifted its head and cried out, 'You shall not have a bride before I get one!'

So the prince returned to the castle and told his parents about the snake on the road. The king didn't understand what was going on, he had never heard of a snake in his kingdom and why should they bother about the snake being married.

'Because he is the firstborn,' said the queen with a big sigh. She told the king and the prince about the old woman with flowers in her hair, the two roses and how she did not know how to choose, and how she had given birth to two children that day, first a little green snake and then the prince. The king and the prince were deeply shocked, but the king understood that the lindorm was right when it said that they had to find a princess for it before the prince could get married.

They found a lovely princess somewhere in the neighbouring kingdom and asked her if she wanted to marry the firstborn of the king and the queen. Her father was very surprised when he was told that there were two brothers. He knew the other prince well and had always been told that he was the only son. He told the king that he would love to have his daughter married to the oldest prince. The king and queen never told the princess who she would be marrying, so the lovely young woman was standing in front of the altar in the church filled with people with some anxiety. The door opened and when she turned around she saw the lindorm slithering towards her. The large green snake crept up next to her and the priest fulfilled the ceremony. The princess's voice trembled when she said her yes, while the lindorm's 'Yes!' was firm and deep. In the evening the couple were left alone in the bedchamber. Next morning when the king and the queen opened the door to the chamber, they were in for a shock. The princess had been torn to pieces by the lindorm. There was blood everywhere but her shift was hanging nicely on a chair. And there was no sign of the lindorm.

A year passed. The prince once more wanted to go out to find a princess. And again the lindorm was lying on the road blocking it for the prince. 'You shall not have a bride before I get one.'

They had to search in one of the kingdoms further away so they had not heard about the first princess. She also wasn't told anything and when she saw her future husband she nearly fainted. In the morning the king and queen opened the door to the wedding chamber. They expected the worst and it had happened again. The princess was torn to pieces and the lindorm was nowhere to be found.

Another year passed. The prince once more wanted to go out to find a princess. And again the lindorm was lying on the road blocking the prince. 'You shall not have a bride before I get one.'

It seemed like there was nothing they could do. The king went hunting and passed the old forester's house. It looked so cosy and nice with a little garden outside the house. The windows were painted in a lovely blue colour. The king knocked on the door and was asked to come in.

'You are doing very well,' said the king, 'and you live here on your own, I understand.'

'Yes, my wife died many years ago,' said the gamekeeper.

'One would never know,' said the king and looked around in the tidy and cosy living room. It was small, but it was a good home.

'My daughter takes care of the house,' said the gamekeeper. 'She works hard every day.'

A lovely young woman came into the living room with two cups of tea for the king and her father. The king stood up and said: 'Would you like to have your daughter marry my son?'

'I have heard about the lindorm,' said the gamekeeper, 'so even though I would love to obey the king in every aspect of my life, I must say no to this one. I love my daughter and I want her to marry someone she can love.'

'I am your king,' said the king, 'and I demand you to give your daughter to be my oldest son's wife.'

The king stood up and left the little cottage.

The gamekeeper sat on the sofa overwhelmed with grief. His daughter came in and asked him why he was so sad. 'You are going to marry his son, the lindorm,' said the gamekeeper.

'What?' she said. 'He is going to tear me apart just like the other two.'

'Yes,' he said, 'but I don't think there is much we can do about it. I am just a poor gamekeeper.'

She walked into the forest and she was so angry. Why should she die just because the king wanted her to do so? If there was only a way for her to defend herself against the monster. She came into a clearing and raised her fist against the sky. She gave a scream of anger and desperation. She fell down to her knees. Then she heard a voice, 'I know what your trouble is and I can help you.'

The gamekeeper's daughter raised her head and saw an old woman standing in front of her. She stood up and said, 'I am going to die just because I am going to be married to a lindorm,' said the gamekeeper's daughter. 'The king has decided that I am going to be sacrificed.'

The old woman told her that there were things to be done about this. 'Get married in the church just like the others,' the old woman said, 'but before you are going into the church you should ask the queen for two large oak barrels to be placed in the wedding chamber. One with strong lye water to cleanse the lindorm and one with milk to soften his skin. And ask for seven stiff brooms. When you enter the wedding chamber, you shall wear nine shifts underneath your wedding dress. And when the lindorm asks you to take off your clothes ask him to take his off first. In the end you will have more shifts than the lindorm has layers of skin.'

The young woman went around in the little village and borrowed eight clean white shifts. On the wedding day she wore the nine shifts under the wedding dress. There was very little of the joy and celebration that one normally connects to a wedding. The priest went quickly through the rituals and then he asked and they both loudly said, 'Yes.'

Before the couple was left alone to spend their wedding night in the wedding chamber the gamekeeper's daughter asked for two big barrels of the finest oak, one filled with the strongest lye possible and the other filled with milk. And seven stiff brooms. The servants laughed at her requests, but the queen defended her. 'I know it sounds crazy. I think it is because she is nervous,' said the queen, 'and she is not used to having servants doing things for her. It is best to get what she is asking for.'

In the wedding chamber the girl took off her wedding dress and the lindorm looked at the beautiful young girl and said, 'Take off your shift.'

'You first!' she said.

'No one has said that to me before,' said the lindorm.

'But I do,' she said. 'You first!'

The lindorm slithered and wiggled and slowly the first layer of snakeskin came off his body. The gamekeeper's daughter took off one of her shifts.

The lindorm saw that she still had a shift on and said, 'Take off your shift.'

'You first!' said the gamekeeper's daughter.

'No one has said that to me before,' said the lindorm.

'But I do,' said the gamekeeper's daughter.

The lindorm slithered and wiggled and slowly the second layer of snakeskin came off his body. The gamekeeper's daughter took another one of her shifts off and she still had one underneath the one she had just taken off.

The lindorm said, 'Take off your shift.'

'You first!' she said.

'No one has said that to me before,' said the lindorm.

'But I do,' she said.

The lindorm slithered and wiggled and slowly the third layer of snakeskin came off his body. The gamekeeper's daughter took another one of her shifts off.

And so it continued, layer after layer until the gamekeeper's daughter stood there naked as when she was born and the lindorm was nothing but a big lump of red meat. The gamekeeper's daughter then took the first broomstick and bade the lindorm in the strong lye while brushing him as hard as she could till the broom was worn out and broken. She did so with all seven brooms and when she was done scrubbing the lindorm there was very little left of him. The gamekeeper's daughter softly held the now small lump of red meat and dipped it gently into the barrel of milk. She crawled into bed and held what was left of the lindorm close to her heart.

In the morning the king, the queen and the gamekeeper entered the wedding chamber expecting the worst. Much to their surprise there was no blood on the walls and no sign of a struggle. Instead the room was full of snakeskins of different sizes and nine nightgowns. There was nothing left of the seven broomsticks and the barrel with the strong soap was red from blood. There was a strong smell of lye and old milk in the room. They stopped in delight when they saw what was in the bed. The gamekeeper's daughter was fast asleep and on her arm was a beautiful young prince sleeping with a happy smile on his face. They left the room in silence. It was long into the day before the two lovebirds came out of the wedding chamber. And so there was a joyful celebration of their wedding.

For seven days and nights the castle was full of joyful dancing. I was there dancing my heels off in my wooden shoes.

After the wedding the lindorm's brother finally went out to search for a princess to marry. He found his fortune in a neighbouring kingdom.

The lindorm later became king and people in the kingdom called him King Lindorm. He and the queen, the gamekeeper's daughter, ruled wisely for many years.

6

THE TWO FRIENDS

Water is essential for humans to survive; so is food and friendship.

There were two friends. One was big and the other was small, and together they were skilled at finding water. They travelled across their entire region with their dowsing sticks seeking water for those in need, and they always found it. Eventually a time came when they had discovered all the water that there was to find. The farmers were happy but once water was found there was no longer any work for the two.

One day the friends heard news that there was a drought in Constantinople and the people desperately needed fresh water. It would be far to travel for the two friends, but they agreed that they needed the work, so they packed their bags, filled two large bundles with food, and off they set.

As they walked, the little friend was struggling with the heavy sack on his back. He tried not to show it, but his big friend could see that he was suffering. The big friend suggested that they should eat the food in the little one's sack to lighten the load. And so they did.

By the time they got to the deep, dark forest of the south the rucksack of the little one was empty and he was relieved of the heavy burden of all that food. He could now easily follow the speedy footsteps of the big one.

When they found a good place to sleep for the night the big friend sat down and unwrapped some food. The little friend sat next to him expecting to be given his share.

'What are you staring at?' said the big friend.

'The food,' said the little friend. 'I am hungry and we have eaten all the food from my rucksack, now it is time for us to eat your share.'

'I never agreed to that,' said the big friend, 'but you can have some of my food. if you give me one of your eyes.'

'What?' said the little friend. 'You can't be serious? I will not give an eye for your food. I shared my food with you for no price.'

'Well,' said the big friend, 'then goodnight.'

A week passed like that with the big friend refusing to share his food. One evening as they sat down and the big friend was getting ready to eat, the little friend had become desperate. He was weak, he was shaking and his stomach was roaring with hunger, so he said to his big friend: 'I'll do it. Take my eye. I just have to eat something.'

The big friend went over to the little friend with his knife and cut out one of the little friend's eyes. 'Now you can have some food,' said the big friend.

The little one filled his belly with food and felt relief, but in his heart he felt grief.

The next day they walked on, and as they came closer to Constantinople, the little one-eyed friend felt hungry again, but again his big friend would not share his food.

'I will only give you food in exchange for your other eye!'

The little friend couldn't bear the thought of being without his sight but the days passed until the hunger became unbearable.

'I have to eat,' said the little friend. 'I can't stand it any more. I will let you take my other eye, but you must then guide me to Constantinople.'

'Very well,' said the big friend, who took out his other eye. The little friend ate and the food felt so good in his hungry belly, but now he was in darkness and was totally dependent on the big friend to guide him.

Evening came and they arrived on a hilltop. The big friend told the little friend to sit and rest against a wooden pole that somebody had raised there. The little blind friend couldn't see that it was a gallows that he was leaning on. The big friend said nothing about the town he could see at the bottom of the hill, but he was sure it was Constantinople.

'Rest here,' said the big friend, 'I will go and find out how far we still have to walk. I will be back later tonight to help you down the hill.' And with that the big friend left the little friend without any intention of coming back.

The little friend could hear his big friend walking down the hill whistling a tune, but the sound became softer and softer until he could no longer hear it. Then suddenly the little friend heard the caw of three ravens who landed above his head.

The first raven shook his feather and said, 'Have you seen how the people of Constantinople suffer? Soon we will have to clean the streets for there will be dead bodies of all kinds. And it is all because the people of Constantinople have forgotten where to find water.'

The second raven gave a 'caw caw' imagining all the inhabitants of Constantinople dying in the streets.

'Where is the water?' asked the third raven.

'You know the old merchant in the little alley next to the palace?' said the first raven. 'He lives in a house with a courtyard and in the middle of that courtyard is a large grey stone. Remove that stone and the fresh water will start flowing.'

'The water coming from that spring is sacred,' said the second raven. 'Especially the first drops of water that come after removing the stone. That water has the power to cure all diseases.'

'Talking of healing water,' said the third raven, 'the dew on the grass around this tree has the power to return your eyesight if you have lost it.'

'Let us fly down to see what is happening in Constantinople,' said the first raven. And so the three ravens flew down to Constantinople. The little friend felt the grass under his feet. The grass was too dry to give him the healing water he needed. He lay down in the grass next to the gallows and fell asleep.

He woke up at the first light of day and the grass was wet. He dabbed the dew in and around his empty eyeholes and slowly he could feel his eyes growing back. After a short time his eyesight had returned and he could see the city of Constantinople in the valley below.

He walked down the hill towards Constantinople to find the old merchant that he'd heard the ravens speak of.

When he found him he told him that he knew where there was a hidden spring in his courtyard. The old merchant walked with the little friend into the courtyard where an enormous grey stone lay in the centre. The little friend was certain that this was the stone the three ravens had talked of. 'We need men with sticks to move this stone,' said the little friend, so the merchant called his servants to come and help.

The little friend found three empty water bottles in the court-yard and when all the old merchant's servants were gathered around the stone the little friend told them to stand in a half circle and get ready to rock the stone. The men pushed and shouted and little by little the stone moved until the first trickle of fresh water began to bubble up from beneath it. The little friend cried, 'Stop pushing!' and he hurried to collect those precious first drops in the three bottles. Then he told the men to continue pushing and soon the stone was completely removed from the mouth of the spring and the fresh water came gushing out, soaking the men. There were joyful cries of 'Water! Water!' and the women came running from all directions with jugs to fill.

The old merchant was delighted. He thanked his little friend and asked him why he had filled the three bottles with the first water. 'This water is very powerful,' said the little friend. 'It can cure all diseases..

'Do you think it can cure my son's blindness?' asked the old merchant.

'I can try,' said the little friend. So he was led inside the merchant's house, where he found the old merchant's son sitting in a chair with the windows wide open listening to the joyful sounds of men and women rushing to collect water. The young man smiled when he heard his father's footsteps.

'There is a young traveller from the north who may be able to cure your blindness,' said the old merchant to his son.

The young man smiled and said, 'I would love to see your face, father.'

The blind son cupped his hand and the little friend poured some water from one of the bottles into it. The blind son gently bathed his blind eyes with the water and slowly colours and shapes began to emerge before him.

'Father,' he said, 'I can see.'

The merchant called for all his servants and some of the women collecting water to witness the miracle. And they all came rushing in, soaking wet from drinking and splashing in the spring, and embraced the merchant's son.

The young man turned to his father. 'What about my sister?' he said. 'When can I see her?'

The little friend looked at the old merchant.

'What sister?' asked the little friend.

'His little sister,' said the old merchant. 'She is very sick with leprosy and it has changed her from the beautiful girl she once was to something hardly human. We had to protect her by locking her inside a cage in the inner courtyard. We didn't want anyone to see her. It was too dangerous, you don't know what people in Constantinople do to people who have leprosy.'

'Maybe I can cure her with this water,' said the little friend, 'it is worth a try.'

The old merchant said, 'Yes, I will ask one of my maids to follow you to the inner court. I hope you can help her.'

The little friend followed the maid into the inner courtyard, where there was a cage. It was dark, so the little friend asked if there were some lights to be lit. A hand covered in red leprous sores lit a candle inside the cage. When the little friend saw the young woman's face he couldn't help it, he gasped. It was horrible, full of red open wounds. The little friend said that he was there to help her. She opened the door to the cage and the little friend told her to pour the water from the bottles on her body to cure herself. He handed her a bottle and turned away; he could hear the sound of her dress dropping to the floor and the water pouring, and after a while, gasps of delight.

'It's gone! My skin is clear!' and she began to laugh with joy.

When the little friend turned around again, the young woman stood right there in front of him with a lovely smile on her face.

'Thank you, stranger,' said the young woman, 'I am grateful for what you have done. Let us find my father.'

'He is right here,' said the little friend and called for the old merchant and his son. The family reunion was as happy as one can imagine.

The little friend stayed with the family and after some months he asked the old merchant's permission to marry his daughter.

'That my friend, you have to ask her about,' said the old merchant with a smile.

The young woman was more than happy to be married to such a kind and clever young man.

The wedding was amazing and when they all sat around the table, the little friend was asked to tell his story. When he finished his story all the guests were deeply shocked.

'Where is this so-called friend of yours?' they asked him.

'I don't know,' the little friend said. 'He didn't find water for your people in Constantinople. But maybe he is doing well.'

'That is not the question,' the guests explained to the little friend. 'He needs to be found and you can then tell us what punishment he shall endure.'

They hunted down the big friend, finding him in the poorest part of the city. He was brought before the little friend. The big friend was shocked to see the little friend doing so well.

'What shall we do with this man that has made you suffer so much?'

'Do what he did to me,' said the little friend. So the big friend lost his eyes and he was placed on the hill next to the gallows. The three ravens landed on the gallows.

'Have you heard that everything we talked about last year has come true?' said the first raven.

'It is like somebody was listening to what we were saying,' said the second raven.

'Let us see if he is still there,' said the third raven.

So they found the big friend sitting blinded by the foot of the gallows. They began to peck at his flesh and by the time the guards returned to see him in the morning, nothing was left but a pile of bones.

7

THE FAT CAT

Tell this story to anyone that likes to repeat a series of images and tell it together with the listeners. Telling this story well is all down to the rhythm of the storyteller.

An old woman was stirring the pot of porridge when her neighbour called her out for a chat. The old woman told the cat to stir the pot while she was out talking to the neighbour. When she got back, the cat had eaten the porridge and the pot.

'Where is the porridge? And the pot? What have you done?' the old woman asked the cat.

'I have been eating the porridge and the pot,' said the cat, 'and now I am going to eat you.'

And the cat ate the old woman. The cat left the house, walked out into the alley and met Tattyshoe.

Tattyshoe said, 'You look very fat, cat, what have you been eating?'

'I have been eating the porridge and the pot and the old woman,' said the cat, 'and now I am going to eat you.' And the cat ate Tattyshoe. The cat walked into the road and met Shinyshoe.

Shinyshoe said, 'You look very fat, cat, what have you been eating?'

'I have been eating the porridge and the pot and the old woman and Tattyshoe,' said the cat, 'and now I am going to eat you.' And the cat ate Shinyshoe.

The cat met a priest with a crooked walking stick. The priest said, 'You look very fat, cat, what have you been eating?'

'I have been eating the porridge and the pot and the old woman and Tattyshoe and Shinyshoe,' said the cat, 'and now I am going to eat you.' And the cat ate the priest.

The cat walked out of the village. In a tree by the road he met five birds in a flock. The birds flew down from the tree and said, 'You look very fat, cat, what have you been eating?'

'I have been eating the porridge and the pot and the old woman and Tattyshoe and Shinyshoe and a priest with a walking stick,' said the cat, 'and now I am going to eat you.' And the cat ate the five birds in a flock.

The cat came to a lake and met seven dancers. The dancers said, 'You look very fat, cat, what have you been eating?'

'I have been eating the porridge and the pot and the old woman and Tattyshoe and Shinyshoe and a priest with a stick and five birds in a flock,' said the cat, 'and now I am going to eat you.' And the cat ate the seven dancers.

The cat walked into a forest and met a lady with a white tail. The lady said, 'You look very fat, cat, what have you been eating?'

'I have been eating the porridge and the pot and the old woman and Tattyshoe and Shinyshoe and a priest with a stick and five birds in a flock and seven dancers by a lake,' said the cat, 'and now I am going to eat you.' And the cat ate the lady with the white tail.

The cat walked further into the forest and met a woodcutter cutting wood. The woodcutter said, 'You look very fat, cat, what have you been eating?'

'I have been eating the porridge and the pot and the old woman and Tattyshoe and Shinyshoe and a priest with a stick and five birds in a flock and seven dancers by a lake and a lady with a white tail,' said the cat, 'and now I am going to eat you.'

'No you won't,' said the woodcutter and he took his axe and cut the cat in half. And out from the cat came a lady with a tail, seven dancers from a lake, five birds in a flock, a priest with a stick, Shinyshoe so shiny, Tattyshoe so tatty and the old woman, the pot and the porridge. The old woman shook her head once, went home and cooked the porridge.

8

THE SEVENSTAR

The Sevenstar is the star formation known as the Pleiades or the Seven Sisters. In Danish the formation is called 'syvstjernen', 'the Sevenstar'. Notice that it is The Sevenstar like the group of stars is one star. This is the story of how The Sevenstar came to be.

Once there was a man who had six sons. The boys grew up to become men and their father explained to them that they needed to find a skill to learn, so they could work for their food and accommodation. The six brothers went out into the world and each one of them learned a skill.

After two years they returned home. Their father looked at the fine young men and asked the oldest, 'What is your skill? What did you learn out there in the world?'

And the oldest told his father that he had learned how to build ships – faster and better than any other ships.

The father nodded. 'That is a good skill,' he said. 'The world needs more good ships.'

Then he looked at the second oldest and asked him, 'What did you learn, second oldest? I hope it is something that can make a father proud of his son.'

The second oldest brother stepped forward and said, 'I have learned how to sail ships, father.'

'Excellent,' said the father, 'then you can sail your oldest brother's ships. I am proud of both of you. Ships and sails and the sea. There is a need for that. Now, what did you learn, third oldest son?'

'I have learned to listen, father,' said the third oldest son, 'I can hear everything in the world, a bird singing in the forest, the noise of the city, a man snoring in his sleep far away.'

'Amazing,' said the father, 'a good listener is something we can all use at one point in our life. Then, tell me, third youngest son, what did you learn out there in the world?'

'I learned how to shoot with a rifle, father,' said the third youngest son, 'I can hit everything, big or small, fast or slow, I always hit it right in the heart'.

'That is so fine, son,' said the father, 'a good marksman is something that can be used by many kings and knights. Well done!

And you, the second youngest of my sons, what skill did you learn?'

'I learned how to climb a mountain, father. I don't care if it is the tallest mountain with snow on top, I will find my way up there within a moment.'

'Climbing mountains,' said the father, 'that is just wonderful. I have always wanted to climb mountains, but I'm too scared of heights. Now you can climb them for me.'

The father turned to the youngest son, who just stood there calmly listening to all his brother's skills and how their father loved what he heard. 'Now, youngest son,' said the father, 'what did you learn?

'To steal, father, I am a master thief,' said the youngest son. The father stared in shock at the youngest son. Then he looked in anger at all the six brothers like they had done something wrong.

'Get out of my house,' he sneered, 'I don't want a pack of thieves in my house. Leave, all of you.'

So they all left the house.

They walked into town and found a cosy inn in a cellar. As they were drinking their beer they noticed that everybody in the inn was crying. 'What is wrong?' said the brothers in unison.

The waitress came with tears in her eyes. 'It is our princess. She has been taken by a troll. An enormous sea troll that lives somewhere in the ocean on an island. We don't know where it is and the ocean is so big, we have no chance of finding her, so our lovely princess is going to be together with a troll for the rest of her life. It is so sad.'

When she looked up from her crying, the six brothers had silently left the inn to go down to the harbour. The oldest brother started building the ship and the third oldest brother was soon busy listening for the princess somewhere in the big ocean. Suddenly he gave a shout. 'I hear them, her voice is like music, like ringing bells even though she is crying. He is ugly even in his voice, it is so gross, aargh! But now I know where to lead the ship.'

The oldest brother shouted from his newly built ship that they should all go aboard. They entered the ship and the next eldest brother manoeuvred it out into the middle of the ocean led by the listener. A heavy storm, rocks in the middle of the sea and a coastline that suddenly appeared out of nowhere, all these challenges were nothing for the ship and the captain leading it safely to the island where the troll had the princess as a prisoner.

In the middle of the island there was a mountain made out of pure glass. The third youngest son, the mountain climber, climbed up that glass mountain like it was a small Danish hill and saw the troll sitting there on a throne burping and shouting while the beautiful princess was crying her heart out. He climbed back down to the ship, explained what they had to do and the youngest brother was placed on the mountain climber's shoulder, who climbed back to the top of the glass mountain and let the master thief climb down inside the mountain. He waited until the troll fell asleep and when its snoring filled the glass mountain, the youngest brother stole the princess from the troll without a sound.

They climbed up to the mountain climber waiting for them at the top of the mountain. He quickly helped the princess down and then his youngest brother. They were all aboard the ship and the next oldest brother stood at the wheel making sure that the rocky seashore never harmed the wonderful ship built by his brother.

The listener said, 'Now the troll is awake and he is asking for the princess. Now he finds out she is gone and now he is coming after her.'

He did not have to say that, they could all see the giant troll flying out of the glass mountain shouting at the six brothers and the princess on the ship. The princess cried, 'If only someone could shoot the troll in his heart, we would have a chance. He is made of flint stone for the rest. But a very little circle around his heart is vulnerable. But look how fast he is flying. It is impossible to hit that little spot.'

The second youngest brother took his rifle and aimed at the troll's heart. The troll was flying through the air at a fantastic speed. The second youngest brother shot the troll with his rifle and hit him right in the heart. The troll exploded in flintstones that spread around the whole world, so if you walk on the beach or dig in your garden, you might find a flintstone. That is from that troll killed by the second youngest brother, therefore saving the princess.

The brothers made their way back to the town of the princess. She looked at the six brothers, each one of them essential for her release from the troll. The ship helped them to her, the next oldest brother found a way around the cliffs and had steered the ship under the storm, the listener heard her and by doing so he told the captain on the ship where to go, the climber climbed a glass mountain nobody had climbed before, the master thief stole her without the troll discovering anything and the shooter hit the troll right in his heart. She found it very hard to choose which brother was the most important in her rescue. She also knew that if she had to make a choice there would be five broken hearts.

They went to sleep. And God in his heaven decided that he would have all that suffering if the princess had to choose. So instead he made them into stars, seven stars in heaven.

This way all six brothers and the princess were able to be together to the end of time.

9

THE SLEDGE

If 'the Sevenstar' was the first fairy tale I told in public, 'the Sledge' was my second. It was like finding an old friend again to read it during the process of writing this book and now I tell it again if someone asks me for a joyful adventure.

Once there was a king who had only one daughter. She was so grumpy and unhappy that nobody had ever seen her laugh. She had grown up to become a fine-looking young woman with a good heart but was always sad, sometimes crying, other times just walking around with a gloomy face saying nothing.

The king was a good king and a fairly happy king who loved to laugh and enjoy himself, but he had started worrying about the health of his only child as it couldn't be healthy to be moping around like that all the time.

So the king said if a prince could make his daughter laugh, he would then have the princess for his wedded wife and the kingdom when the old king died. Many princes tried, but there was not a glimmer of a smile to be seen on the princess's face.

The king was soon tired of all the princes running around in the castle telling jokes, making faces and other stupid things intended to make the princess laugh. But mostly he was sad because no one could succeed in making his daughter smile.

It wasn't possible to rule a kingdom with all these foolish men running around, so the king proclaimed that if a young man failed to make his daughter laugh, they would be rolled in tar and dipped in feathers. That helped.

In the kingdom there was a man who had three sons, Peder, Paul and Jesper.

Peder could tell jokes so funny that everybody in the local inn would laugh their heads off, so he told his mother and father that he would find his way up to the castle and tell a joke to the princess to make her laugh just as much as the men down in the inn. His mother gave him a big bag of food and his father gave him a wallet full of money.

On his way he met an old woman dragging a sledge. The old woman asked for some food and maybe a penny for the road. Peder said that there was only enough food and money for him.

'It is not going to be a good journey!' the old woman said.

Peder didn't care about the old woman and found his way up to the castle. He was brought into a courtyard, where he found the king and the princess. He told one joke after another and he thought it went very well, but the princess just looked even more sad, so Peder was rolled in tar and dipped in feathers and chased out of the castle. It took his mother half of her butter to remove all the tar from him.

What went wrong for Peder didn't have to be the same for Paul. He was a singer and he knew a lot of funny songs, so he wanted to seek his fortune and he was convinced that he could make the princess laugh. His mother also gave him a bag of food and his father gave him a wallet full of money.

On his way he met an old woman dragging a sledge. She asked for some food and maybe a penny for the road. Paul, like his brother, said that there was only enough food and money for him.

'It is not going to be a good journey,' the old woman said.

Paul didn't care and found his way up to the castle. He sang all his funny songs for the princess, but she started crying in the middle of his best one, so Paul was rolled in tar and dipped in feathers and chased out of the castle. It took his mother the other half of her butter to remove all that tar from him.

Now Jesper said that he would try his luck. 'And what can you do to make her laugh?' asked his father. 'You have never told a joke or sung a funny song in your life.'

That could be,' said Jesper. 'But I will try anyway.' His mother gave him some dry bread and his father only gave him a few pennies for the road.

So Jesper went on his way towards the castle. After a while he sat down and started gnawing on the pieces of the dry bread crusts. An old woman dragging a sledge sat down next to him and asked if he could give her some food and maybe a penny for the road. Jesper gave her what was left of the dry bread crusts and half of the pennies he had from his father.

'It is all I have,' Jesper said with a smile.

'Where are you going?' asked the old woman.

'To the king's castle to make the princess laugh, so I can win her heart and the whole kingdom when the old King dies.'

'Do you know how you will make her laugh?' said the old woman.

'No,' said Jesper, 'I will find out when I get there.'

'You are a kind man,' said the old woman, 'who shared your food and the little money you had. I will help you. You shall have my sledge with the little bird.'

Jesper saw that there was a wooden carved bird on the sledge. 'When you sit on the sledge and say "Pip, little bird!" it will run with you till you say stop. And if someone touches the sledge, the bird will say "Pip" and you just have to say "Hold fast" and they will be stuck to the sledge till you say "Let go!" Take good care of your new sledge and then I think you will make the princess laugh.'

Jesper thanked her and sat on the sledge, said 'Pip, little bird' and off he went with a speed like he was driven by the fastest horses. People were staring as they saw him whizzing by. In the evening he stopped at an inn to get a bed for the night. People couldn't believe their eyes when they saw the speedy sledge pull up outside. Jesper spent his last pennies on a room in the inn and took his sledge with him into his room and tied it to his bed.

He fell asleep at once. One of the young women working at the inn couldn't help it, she just had to take a closer look at the sledge. In the middle of the night, dressed only in her shift, she opened the door to Jesper's room as quietly as possible and looked at the sledge and imagined that she was driving as fast as Jesper had done when he drove into the inn that evening. She couldn't resist it, she just had to touch it. But the moment she did, the bird said, 'Pip!', waking Jesper, who immediately said 'Hold fast!' and then went back to sleep. So she was stuck to the sledge. Later another young woman who worked at the inn did the same. Came in only dressed in her shift and touched the sledge.

'Pip,' said the bird.

'Hold fast!' said Jesper. And then she was stuck.

In the morning there was a third young maiden stuck to the sledge. Jesper set off from the inn with the three maidens running behind each wearing only a shift. The innkeeper ran after him crying, 'Stop! You have three of my best workers stuck to your sledge!' but Jesper just waved and said, 'Farewell'.

Jesper, the sledge and the three maidens, passed a church. The priest stood outside with the degn and they were preparing the sermon for the Sunday service. He knew the three maidens as good churchgoers even though they worked in the godless inn, but this was outrageous. On a Sunday chasing a young man like that. He had to stop it, so he reached out and caught one of the maidens by her shift.

'Pip,' said the bird.

'Hold fast!' said Jesper. And so the priest was now stuck to the maiden.

When the degn saw the priest running after three maidens like that, and on a Sunday just before the church service, he couldn't believe his eyes. He shouted, 'Priest, control yourself. Remember it is Sunday!'

The degn ran after the priest and got hold of his cassock.

'Pip,' said the bird.

'Hold fast!' said Jesper. And so the degn was stuck to the priest.

In this town there was also a blacksmith. He was busy shoeing a horse. When he saw the sledge with Jesper on, and the three maidens, the priest and the degn running after the sledge, he just had to laugh. And a blacksmith in those days would never lose a chance to make a degn look even more foolish, so the blacksmith took his tong and grabbed the degn's trousers. 'Pip,' said the bird. 'Hold fast!' said Jesper. And so ...

The blacksmith had a bundle of hay in his hand from shoeing the horse and when Jesper drove the sledge into a goose farm, seven geese flew up and wanted to eat the delicious hay. 'Pip,' said the bird. 'Hold fast!' said Jesper.

When Jesper drove the sledge into the castle, the princess was sitting by the window sighing with grief. The king was walking up and down the corridors expressing his deep sorrows. The whole castle was filled with sighs and crying. Then suddenly they heard a commotion in the courtyard. The princess and the king ran to the window and when they looked out, they couldn't believe their eyes. On a sledge running like it was driven by seven fast horses sat a young man, Jesper. Behind him were three maidens in shifts, behind them a priest trying to explain himself, behind the priest ran a degn trying to escape the blacksmith's tongs that had a good grip of his trousers. The blacksmith was trying to get rid of the geese eating all his hay. It was a sight for gods and all the courtiers of the castle, the cook, the servants, the maids, came out to see the spectacle and they all had a good laugh.

In the window sat the princess staring at the turmoil. First she started to smile, and after a while she gave a little outburst of joy and then she just let go. It was too hilarious to watch the faces of all of these people running after Jesper and the birds made such horrible screams and the whole thing was just so bizarre, she burst into fits of laughter.

Jesper saw it, cried, 'Stop!' and they all stopped.

Then he said, 'Let go!' and the maidens ran home to the inn to get dressed, the priest and the degn ran back to the church, the priest gave an inspired sermon and the blacksmith went back to shoe the horse.

The seven geese were brought back to the farm with a warning that the meat from them might soon be wanted for a wedding celebration.

Jesper stood in the courtyard calling to the princess, 'I made you laugh.'

And she just said, 'Yes, and I know you are going to make me laugh again.'

The king was overjoyed and he invited Jesper into the castle.

Jesper and the not-so-grumpy-any-more-princess got married and Jesper often took her for long rides on the sledge. And every day he made her laugh.

10

A FATHER'S HEART

Short and deep, I love this story for its richness even if it is one of
the shortest stories in the collection.

Once there was a man who had three sons. On his farm there was
a forest.

The man became very sick and was going to die. The oldest
son came to him and asked him if he had any plans for the forest
after his death.

'I want you to have all the tall trees and the low trees,' said the
dying man.

The oldest son thought about it. He smiled and said to himself, 'If I am going to inherit the tall trees and the low trees I am
going to inherit all the trees in the forest. That means I am going
to inherit the whole forest.' He danced as he walked away from
his father.

The middle brother came into the bedroom of his father and asked him about the forest.

'I want you to have all the thin trees and the thick ones,' said the dying man.

The middle brother nodded and smiled. That was all fine. He knew he was going to inherit the whole forest.

When the youngest brother came to see his father, the old man was very ill. His breath was short and he was lying in his bed hardly able to smile at the youngest of the three sons.

The youngest brother took his father's hand and held it for a while. Then he asked,

'What is going to happen with the forest when you are dead, Father?'

'I want you to have all the straight trees and all the bent trees,' said the dying man.

'I will make sure your wishes are fulfilled,' said the youngest brother, he too believing that his father had given him the whole forest.

The youngest son kissed his father and left.

Not long after, the old man died.

They buried their father in the graveyard, and then the three brothers met with a solicitor.

The oldest brother stepped forward. 'The forest is mine,' he said. 'I was told by my father that I should have all the tall trees and all the low trees. And that is, as we all know, all the trees in the forest.'

'No!' said the middle brother. 'Father told me that I should have all the thin trees and all the thick trees in the forest. And that is all the trees in the forest.'

'Well,' said the youngest of the brothers, 'our father told me that I should have all the bent trees and all the straight trees. What should we do to honour our father's wishes?'

'I have a solution,' said the solicitor. 'We are going to dig up the body of your father and tie him to a tree. You will then shoot at his heart and the one that hits closest to the heart is going to have the forest.'

And so it was, they dug up the body of the old man and the body was tied to one of the trees in the forest. The three brothers were each given a gun.

The two oldest brothers aimed their guns at their dead father.

The youngest just stood there, paralysed.

'I can't do it,' he said. 'My father has always been a good father to me, and even if he is dead I can't make myself shoot at his heart.'

The solicitor stepped forward and stopped the two oldest brothers before they could take a shot at the dead man.

He looked at the youngest brother and smiled.

'You hit your father right in his heart,' he said, 'and you shall have the forest.'

11

THE PRINCESS
WHO BECAME A MAN

When you read this story, be with somebody that you trust and if one of the mental images it creates bothers you, talk about it and find a way to make it a useful experience for you.

Once in a kingdom far away there was a king and a queen. The queen gave birth to a lovely daughter and the love between the three grew every day. Some years later the queen became very sick and soon after, she died. When the king stood at her graveside he said, 'As you know, my love, a king needs a queen and I will look for another wife somewhere in my kingdom. But I will make sure that the new queen is as beautiful as you were.'

And so the king searched for a new queen. He looked everywhere in his kingdom, in the mountains and the glens, in the countryside and in the towns. He was introduced to all the lovely eligible women in his kingdom and beyond, from fine princesses to poor fishermen's daughters. But there was no one as beautiful as the queen, who was now long dead in her grave.

The king returned home and walked the halls of his castle feeling low. He passed the dressing room of the queen. In front of a mirror stood a young woman wearing a beautiful golden dress. The king was stunned. This woman was as beautiful or even more beautiful than the queen. He cried out, 'I have finally found her, the woman that I am going to marry. You are as beautiful as the queen I buried a long time ago.'

The woman in front of the mirror was the princess, now a young woman, who was trying on one of her mother's dresses and it fitted perfectly. Horrified, she looked at the king and said, 'But father, I am your daughter and a father can't marry his own daughter.'

The king stared at the princess and said, 'I am the king in this castle and a king can marry who he likes and I will marry you. Be prepared to be my wife this Saturday.'

The king left the princess sobbing in the queen's dressing room.

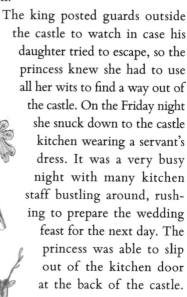

The king posted guards outside the castle to watch in case his daughter tried to escape, so the princess knew she had to use all her wits to find a way out of the castle. On the Friday night she snuck down to the castle kitchen wearing a servant's dress. It was a very busy night with many kitchen staff bustling around, rushing to prepare the wedding feast for the next day. The princess was able to slip out of the kitchen door at the back of the castle.

On her way out she had grabbed a large kitchen knife for protection should the king try to bring her back with force.

The kitchen door led out to a small wooden bridge, where servants were busy carrying barrels of beer, vegetables and meat for the wedding. She followed the stream of servants across the bridge. 'If I could only find my way into the forest I will be safe,' she thought to herself and started running as fast as she could across the field.

But alas it was a full moon and the king's guards spotted her.

'There she is,' a cold voice shouted out.

The king heard the cry and shouted to his two hunting dogs, 'Get her back! Before she slips into the forest!'

The two wild, black beasts as big as ponies barked and snapped into the night as they chased after the princess.

She could hear the hounds getting closer and closer. And when she turned she saw two wild beasts with blood in their eyes running so fast she knew she would have to think quickly. They were going to catch her before she could find her way into the safety of the forest. The two dogs could smell her fear and snarled at her. They were so close their white teeth were ready to dig deep into her flesh and drag her back to the castle. She quickly tore open her dress and with the kitchen knife she sliced off one of her breasts and tossed it to one dog, then quickly cut off the second breast and threw it to the other dog, satisfying their thirst for blood. She then turned and ran into the forest hearing the sound of the dogs savagely eating her breasts and the distant cries of her father.

The princess stumbled into the forest. Blood poured from her wounds and as she walked along the forest path she became weaker and weaker. She fell to her knees and collapsed on the soft moss of the forest floor.

She woke up to the smell of soup. She was lying in a bed in a little wooden hut and her wounds had been bandaged. An old man was calmly stirring a pot and he turned to her and smiled when he sensed her eyes upon him. 'Ah, you're awake.'

'Did you do this?' she asked him and pointed to the bandages.

'Yes I did,' he said. 'You would have died if I had not stopped the bleeding. I've used herbs to make sure that the wounds will not be infected. Now you need to eat something to get your strength back.'

He brought her soup and bread. She ate and the old man sat by the window. When she had finished she looked around. On a chair were some green clothes fit for a marksman.

'Your clothes were torn and covered in blood, so I burned them. These hunting clothes are all I have. I think they will fit you when you are well enough, but now you must rest.'

The days passed and when she was stronger she dressed herself in the hunting clothes, which fitted her perfectly and were more comfortable than any dress she had ever worn.

When she was ready the old man took her outside and gave her a rifle. 'I will teach you everything I know,' he said, and showed her first how to handle a rifle. The old man then taught her how to hunt hare, pheasant and wild boar. Finally he taught her how to hunt deer, the finest prey in the forest. After a while her skill became so refined that whatever she aimed at, big or small, fast or slow, she always hit the target right in the heart.

One day the old man said, 'You are now ready to go out into the world. There is a kingdom on the other side of the forest. Find the castle and tell them that you are a marksman and you are seeking work. And if you ever find yourself in danger, think of me and I will help you.'

The old man gave her his finest most manly clothes and she set off to the new kingdom.

The new marksman's arrival at the castle on the other side of the forest couldn't have been more timely. The king was thrilled as he was in need of a new marksman to accompany him on his hunts. When they set out into the forest the king saw just what an incredible shooter this new marksman was. Whatever beast the marksman aimed at he always shot it right in the heart.

The king had a daughter, and she was intrigued by the new marksman. She invited him to the castle, and they became friends. When she asked her father if she could marry the new marksman, the king could think of no finer husband for his dear daughter and he agreed.

But it was not all going to be that simple. In the castle there was a knight called the Red Knight. He had long wanted to marry the princess and when he heard about the wedding of the new marksman and the princess, he was so full of envy he began scheming ways to bring evil upon the marksman.

The wedding was an absolute joy for all and when the princess and the marksman went to their wedding chamber to spend their first night together all the guests wished them well.

Once alone in the bed the marksman could no longer keep his secret and confessed to his beloved that he had the body parts of a woman and was once a princess like her. The marksman told his story and when he had finished the princess smiled and kissed her true love, saying, 'It does not matter one bit to me. I love you completely just as you are.'

The princess and the marksman had a night together like no other they had known. When they fell asleep the door to their closet opened and out crept the Red Knight, who had witnessed everything.

The next morning when the king and all the guests opened the door to their bed chamber to congratulate them on their first night together the Red Knight was there as well.

He stepped forward and said, 'It is beautiful to see that a couple of the same sex can love one another.'

Nobody took any notice of him except the king and when they were alone the king asked the Red Knight what he meant. The knight told him that the marksman was a woman and advised him to seek proof by inviting everyone in the castle to bathe in the lake that morning.

And so all the guests and courtiers ran down to the lake, took off their clothes and jumped in the water. The marksman stood at the edge of the lake, slowly removing his socks and taking time to fold them. The king and the Red Knight were watching from the water.

'Are you scared to take off your clothes?' called the Red Knight.

Knowing he was in danger, the new marksman thought upon the old man and suddenly out of the forest came a stag. It charged into the lake where everyone was bathing. The king called out 'Catch it! Catch it!' to the marksman. The stag charged from the lake, up the banks and over a hilltop. The marksman chased after it.

On the other side of the hill the stag was nowhere to be seen, but instead there stood an old tree, and from behind that tree came the old man. 'The stag is gone, no need to chase it any more. You are a man now and you can bathe with everyone in the lake without fear. But one thing you must promise me. Your first born child will be mine. Bring the baby to me in the forest.'

The marksman promised and returned to the lake. He told the king that the stag had been too fast and he was gone. He then took off all his clothes and jumped in the lake, and much to the king's relief the marksman appeared to be a man.

When the princess learned that the marksman was now a man she was filled with joy at the prospect of them having a child. But that joy was short-lived when she learned of the marksman's promise to the old man. When their first child was born, the thought of giving it up broke their hearts, but the princess said to her beloved marksman, 'A promise is a promise, and we must do as the old man asked.'

The marksman wrapped the baby in a cloth and carried it to the old man's hut in the forest. When the old man saw the child he said, 'Come outside with me to the chopping block and take one leg of your child.' The marksman did so and the old man took the other leg and cut the baby to the belly.

'Did that hurt?' asked the old man.

'Yes' said the trembling marksman with tears streaming down his face.

'So I was hurt the day you stood in your mother's dress and your father desired to marry you.'

Then the old man cut the baby all the way to the head.

'Did that hurt you?' asked the old man.

'Yes, that hurt me,' said the marksman.

'So I was hurt when you cut off your breasts and fed them to the hounds.'

Then the old man cut the baby's head into two halves.

'Did that hurt you?'

'Yes.'

The old man took the two halves of the boy. 'Wait here a while,' he said to the marksman and he went inside. A moment after he came out with a large platter.

'Don't open the lid,' said the old man. 'Take it to your wife but do not open the lid before you arrive home with it.'

The new marksman did as he was told. He went home to his princess and told her to expect the worst. She lifted the lid of the platter and inside there was her smiling, beautiful baby boy, sound and well as before.

12

THREE LESSONS
TO BE LEARNED

A giant knows things we have forgotten.

Once there was a farmer who had three daughters.

One day a huge man came driving into the farmyard in a golden coach with six black horses in front. He asked for the hand of one of the daughters. Maren was the eldest of the three. The huge man asked her if she would be his wife, she accepted and sat next to him on the golden coach and they drove out of the farm.

A year passed and another huge man in a golden coach with six white horses came, and he asked for permission to marry the next daughter, Karen. She sat next to him as they drove out.

A year passed and the youngest daughter, Mette, was asked by a huge man in a golden coach with six grey stallions, so now all three daughters were well on their way.

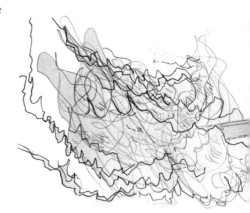

One day the old man wanted to see his daughters and he began with the first, Maren.

When he arrived, Maren told her father that her husband was a giant and that he looked after her well. After talking for a while they needed something to eat and her husband said that they could make some strong blood barley soup. So the giant told Maren to follow him out to the barn. There the giant smashed his head against a wooden post holding the roof. Blood poured out of the giant's head and Maren was busy catching the blood, so she could use it in the soup. The old man thought it was a lovely way to get blood for blood barley soup.

He said farewell and drove to Karen.

She had also married a giant. They wanted to serve some fish for the guest and the giant told Karen that they could get some out in the lake close by. So they rowed out with a big basket for the fish.

The giant asked Karen, 'Are my eyes red?'

'No,' Karen said.

A little bit longer out towards the middle of the lake.

'Are my eyes red?' asked the giant.

'No,' Karen said.

A little bit further and it looked like they were in the middle of the lake.

'Now, are my eyes red?' said the giant.

'Yes,' Karen said and her husband jumped into the water with the basket. When he came up, it was full of fish. It was a lovely meal they shared with all that fish. The old man thought it was a lovely skill to know how to catch fish like that.

He said farewell and went to his youngest daughter, Mette.

He arrived late at Mette's house. She told her father that the giant was kind and took good care of her. As it was getting dark outside Mette asked her husband if he could light some candles.

'Can you get me some embers from the fire?' asked the giant, and Mette brought him some. The giant placed them on his fingers and the fingers lit like candles and they had a wonderful evening together in the light of the candles. The old man thought that it was a lovely skill to know.

Once back in his own house the old man told his wife that they should have barley blood soup.

The old man's wife said, 'Where do you think you will get that blood from? We have no animal to slaughter and we can't afford to buy it at the butcher.'

'Just wait and see, follow me to the barn,' he said. 'Bring a big pot.'

Inside the barn he told his wife to be ready with the big pot. Then he started banging his head against one of the posts in the barn. Nothing happened except that the old man had to go to bed with a headache. The bulge from the attempt to get some blood was visible for several days.

Once out of bed he told his wife to bring a basket. They were going to fish in the big lake. And so they went out in their little rowing boat. 'Look here,' the old man said to his wife, 'are my eyes red?'

'No,' his wife said, 'they are just like they always are, not red at all.'

They rowed further out towards the middle of the lake.

'Are my eyes red now?'

'No,' his wife said, 'what is this all about?'

The old man just told her to say that his eyes were red and a little bit further out on the lake he asked her, 'Are my eyes red now?'

'Yes,' she said dutifully, 'they are red now.'

So the old man jumped into the ice cold lake with the basket. When he came up again, the basket was empty and he was shivering with cold.

His wife said, 'Why do you have to behave like a giant? You are no giant!'

At night his wife wanted to light a candle, so they could see what they were doing.

'Don't waste the expensive candle. I will show you something,' said the old man.

He told her to bring some embers, so she took a shovel and brought him some. 'Now look!' he said and took the burning hot embers and placed them on his fingers. He screamed as the burning embers burned his fingers and there was no light on any of them. His wife just shook her head and went to light a candle in the normal way. With his hands in cold water and a face that expressed the pain from his burning wounds, he looked so miserable.

'Why did you do that?' his wife said.

'Because my son-in-law did it,' he said.

'But you are no giant and you will never be a giant,' said his wife. 'That is just the way it is.'

The old man had learned a lesson three times and had learned it the hard way. He and his wife visited their daughters many times after that, but the old man was no longer interested in any of the magical skills his three sons-in-law possessed.

13

THE HIGH CHURCH OF LUND

St Laurentis is the Swedish word for St Lawrence. He is the patron saint of comedians and cooks. It is said that the shooting stars of the Perseid meteor shower are St Lawrence's tears, either of pain or of laughter.

It was in the days of Odin. People from the town of Lund were worshipping Freya in the spring, her brother Freyr in the autumn, and if they needed help in warfare they asked Thor.

Outside the town was a green hill covered in grass. When the sun had set, the hill came alive. A huge gate suddenly appeared and out came a giant. Every night the giant opened the gate and went hunting either in the forests or by the sea. He only hunted at night because if he was hit by a sunbeam, he would turn into stone.

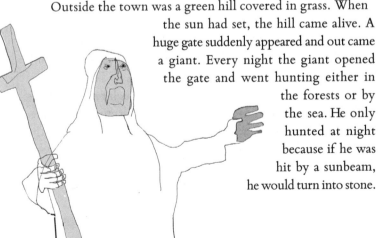

During the night he ran into the forests to catch deer and wild boar, he went to the sea and landed cod and occasionally a whale, and he plucked owls from the sky. In the morning before sunrise he came home with food for his family.

To the town came a monk; St Laurentius was his name. He came from Rome and he wanted to change the faith and beliefs of the people of Lund. Odin and Thor and all the other gods should be replaced by one god and his son. In the beginning it was hard for the people to grasp these new ideas of only one god and his son that died on a cross. St Laurentius was patient and his words slowly started to resonate. There was something about his eyes when he started talking about the new religion. It was as if they were shining like stars in the sky.

The stories started to resonate with the people of Lund and soon they were spreading all over the town. And the crowd grew every Sunday until it was packed with people and it was time to find a bigger space. St Laurentius told the crowd, his congregation as he called it, that next Sunday they would meet on the green hill just outside Lund.

Next Sunday afternoon a huge crowd had gathered on the hill just outside Lund. They sat on the grass and St Laurentius stood by the foot of the hill talking, his eyes sparkling and his words like fire. The sun setting in the west made the picture of fire even more real. The crowd loved every word St Laurentius said, when suddenly there was a rumbling from the other side of the hill. The sun had just set and the giant was getting ready to hunt. He opened the big gate and stepped outside. Much to his surprise his hill was full of people and he gave a giant grunt when he saw them. The crowd screamed in horror, panicked and ran down the hill back into the town. Only St Laurentius didn't move. He stood there firmly and looked at the giant.

'Why did you do that? You scared my flock, there was no reason for that,' said St Laurentius.

'I always go hunting now that the sun is gone and I didn't mean to scare anyone, but people are afraid of me, because I am so big. Why are you not scared of me?' said the giant.

'I trust God, and therefore nothing bad can happen to me,' said St Laurentius.

'Why don't you just find another place to talk to all these people?' said the giant, 'so I can crawl in and out of my home without people screaming and running away when they see me.'

'We don't have a cathedral,' said St Laurentius.

'A what?' said the giant.

'A big building large enough to hold my entire congregation,' said St Laurentius. 'If I had a cathedral to call my own, I could indeed make wonders. I would convince all the people of Lund that there is only God, and his son died for them.'

'You know your eyes shine like the stars in the sky when you speak about this one God thing,' said the giant. 'I could build a cathedral for you.'

'Would you?' said St Laurentius.

'All I want is your eyes,' said the giant.

'What?' said St Laurentius in shock, 'I can't give you my eyes.'

There was a moment of silence and then the giant said, 'If you guess my name, I will build that cathedral for nothing. But if you don't, I shall have your shining eyes for my son.'

St Laurentius thought about how hard it could be to guess a giant's name, so he agreed.

And the giant started that same night. He ran up into the rocky slopes north of the town and started cutting large bricks out of the granite there. Back in town he started piling these bricks on top of the others.

Meanwhile, St Laurentius said, 'Your name is Svend.'

'No,' said the giant.

'Peter? Niels? Rasmus?' said St Laurentius.

'No,' said the giant, and so it continued all night long.

St Laurentius tried all the names he knew, Mikkel, Vagn, Søren, Nikolaj, Andreas, Torben, Hans, etc. And the giant didn't say anything to these names, just shook his head and after a while not even that. When the sun rose in the sky, the giant was back inside his hill and St Laurentius was making a list of possible names.

In the night the giant hunted food for his family, made these massive bricks and placed the bricks into the cathedral construction while St Laurentius ran after him saying all the names he had gathered during the day.

Summer went like that and in August the cathedral was nearly finished, it was a big and in many ways beautiful cathedral. It was exactly like St Laurentius wanted it and he should have been happy. But he was not, because he knew that the next morning after the giant had finished building the cathedral he would have to give the giant his eyes. He walked out of town up on the hill to have one last glimpse of the stars in the dark. He cried and with tears rolling down his cheeks he went down on his knees and quietly said a prayer to save his eyes. He felt the soft grass on his forehead as it touched the ground and slowly he turned so it was his cheek and ear that felt the green grass. He was lying there looking out into the darkness. Then he heard a voice from inside the hill, it was the wife of the giant speaking. 'Wake up, little one, it is soon time for your father to come back with the shining eyes of St Laurentius. Your father has told me many times that the eyes of St Laurentius are the most beautiful eyes in the world and because your father is so smart, you will have them when he gets home. And the sun will soon rise so it is time for your father Finn to come home.'

St Laurentius sat up. He ran down the hill into town, where the giant was about to put the last stone on the cathedral.

He heard St Laurentius coming down towards him while shouting, 'Your name is Finn, your name is Finn, you have built the beautiful cathedral for free, thank you for that.'

When Finn understood that he had done all that work for nothing he gave a cry of anger and threw the last stone far out into the farmland of Scania, where to this day you can find a stone cut into a brick. Finn then ran down into the basement of the cathedral and wrapped his arms around one of the pillars. He was just about to tear the cathedral to the ground when, in that moment, he was hit by the first light of the sun and he became stone.

If you go to Lund and walk down into the crypt you will see Finn, or rather StoneFinn. He is still embracing the pillar in the middle of the crypt.

For many years St Laurentius held his sermons in the cathedral in Lund and his eyes were still shining on his last days here on earth.

If you ask me what happened to Finn's wife and son, I have no certain knowledge. It is said that they followed the gods Odin, Freya and Thor up north as they were chased out of Denmark, but I think that is just a rumour.

14

THE DANISH CAPTAIN

When I walked inside the church in Angelstad in Småland, Sweden, the first thing that caught my eye was two Danish flags. They were placed on top of a black shield and in between the two Danish flags lay an old sword. I read the inscription on the shield:

'In memory of the Danish captain who was arquebused (shot with a musket) near Hylte second day of Christmas 1570. He was faithful in death as well in life. Given to the church by 'The Danish Ladies' 1873'.

I looked around to see if there was anyone who could solve the mystery for me. Nobody was there, so I took a picture of the shield and drove back to the festival. Back home in Denmark I did some research. Apparently, the Danish Captain was two hours late for the departure of the Danish soldiers leaving Småland for their return to Denmark after the Nordic Seven Years War. He was therefore executed. The story had been drawing headlines in the Danish magazine *Illustrated Times* back in 1873, and the collective of ladies, 'De Danske Damer' gave the shield to the church in Angelstad.

There were a lot of questions in my mind and this story is my suggestion to answer some of these questions.

In Annerstad, a small town about ten miles south of Angelstad, the priest's daughter Hilda had fallen in love with a Danish captain. Hilda had heard the many rumours that soldiers from Denmark were savages who were raping and stealing their way around Småland, but she was a free minded young woman and not one to believe in rumours. Hilda first saw her captain one beautiful summer's evening, when she was on her way home from visiting Margretha, her best friend, who lived with her mother and father in the forest not far from Lake Bolmen.

On her way home, she walked down to Lake Bolmen to get a glimpse of the beautiful sunset and its flickering lights on the water. And there he was. She stood there for a long time, gazing at the tall, handsome man leaning against a tree in the red light of the setting sun. He was singing songs from his homeland. A brown horse was tied to another tree nearby. She watched until the sun had gone down. Then it was getting a little cold, so she turned to leave and a twig cracked under her foot. The man looked over and when he saw her, he smiled softly and asked her if she would like him to escort her home. She accepted and, seeing she was cold, he placed his woollen military coat over her shoulders and invited her to sit upon the horse while he led it on foot. He walked the horse all the way to the priest's farm in Annerstad and there he helped her down from his horse. He promised to come back another day, and he did.

Twice a week he visited Hilda, and started attending her father's church. Their love grew, and when six months had passed, they celebrated their engagement. Hilda's father had given his blessing, but to the people of Annerstad this was an outright scandal! They had accused the priest and his daughter of fraternising with the enemy. Nevertheless, the Danish captain and Hilda planned to marry as soon as this nonsensical war was over.

Rumours of a peace treaty being negotiated had been circulating for months. It was clear that the war was coming to an end. The Danish king was bankrupt, and the Swedish king had gone mad. Finally, on 13th December 1570, a peace treaty was signed in Stettin in what is now Poland. The remaining Danish soldiers were making their final preparations to leave Småland.

December 24th, Christmas Eve, was the highlight of the year in churches of the Nordic countries. A celebration of the birth of Christ would normally have filled a church, and there would be people standing outside. But nothing was normal in times of war.

It was nearly 5 o'clock, snow was gently falling, and Hilda was on her way to her father's church in Annerstad. Beside her walked her best friend, Margretha with her family. As they walked, the two girls whispered to each other.

'Your engagement party was so much fun. He is a wonderful man, your Danish Captain.' whispered Margretha.

'Thank you for coming,' said Hilda. 'I am finding out who my real friends are.'

They giggled softly and Hilda held Margretha's arm a little tighter.

'Thank you for bringing your family tonight.' whispered Hilda.

'It wasn't easy. My father first refused saying you are a family of traitors, but I told him how much you like your captain and that he is a good man. Then my father said it was fine, as long as this captain didn't speak to them in Danish.'

Hilda laughed and looked at Margretha's father, a proud woodcutter. He looked straight ahead as he and his wife came up to the church. There they were greeted by the Danish Captain who told them how happy he was to see them all. He did it in perfect Swedish with a little twist of the local accent. Margretha's father couldn't help smiling just a bit.

Though the church was half full, the priest delivered the Christmas service with passion. Reminding all of the king who brought peace to Judea, and encouraging the people of Angelstad to pray for peace in their hearts as this terrible war was coming to an end.

The priest suggested that when the Danish soldiers leave Småland, the people of Annerstad should stand by the roadside and say farewell in a friendly and decent manner. By doing so, they would pave the way for a future relationship between the Danes and the Swedes based on kindness and Christian love.

It was a good service and when the priest stepped down the Danish Captain thanked him for his words. He agreed, it was just a question of time before peace between the two nations would be a reality.

Later that evening at the priest's house, Hilda's mother had made the Christmas dinner: a duck given by the Danish Captain, with potatoes, nuts and green kale. It was a feast in these hard times when food had been scarce.

The priest asked the captain when the Danish soldiers were to be evacuated.

'We will depart on the second day of Christmas,' said the Danish Captain, 'but I will return to Annerstad as soon as I possibly can.' Hilda smiled at the thought of her beloved coming back to be with her.

The Christmas games commenced, and the night was full of joy and hope for the future and the Danish Captain slept in the guest bedroom.

On the morning of the first day of Christmas he returned to the barracks in Hylte to inform his men of their departure procedure the following day. Although the general had ordered the regiment to depart the barracks by 10 o'clock on the second day of Christmas, the captain wanted to make the most of his last hours with Hilda, so he informed his men that they would depart at twelve o'clock on the second day of Christmas. The men were pleased at the prospect of having a little more time in bed after Christmas celebrations, and it wasn't as if the general ever showed up at the barracks, so no-one was concerned.

He packed up his things so he would be ready to set off the next morning, and then he returned to the priest's house to make the most of his final day with Hilda, bringing with him his friend, a lieutenant. Margretha came along too and the first day of Christmas again was a day of food, games and laughter. The lieutenant, however, did not seem as spirited as the rest of the party, and both Hilda and Margretha did not trust his nature.

Later that evening the priest said to the captain,

'You are welcome to stay again but you probably have to get back to the barracks ready for your departure tomorrow.'

The captain smiled and said, 'It won't be a problem for me to stay one last night here. I have arranged it all. My men and I will be departing at 12 o'clock tomorrow so we can enjoy the morning before I bid you all farewell.' The lieutenant however, said goodnight to the captain and his hosts, and went back to the barracks.

It was approaching 12 o'clock on the second day of Christmas and the captain arrived at the barracks. To his horror, he saw the general standing glaring at him with rage in his eyes. He had arrived late the previous night and had ordered the men to be ready to leave at the agreed time of ten o'clock. So, the men had been waiting for the captain for two hours when he finally appeared.

'What is the reason for this delay? Why are you two hours late when we have to depart from this godforsaken place?' said the general.

'I can explain,' said the Danish Captain, 'I wasn't here yesterday evening and this morning because I was with the priest in Annerstad.'

'And what were you doing with the priest?' said the general.

'Talking about how wonderful it is going to be when peace is here, and we can meet in friendship, Danes and Swedes,' said the Danish Captain.

'You are fraternising with the enemy. Your lieutenant has told me everything and here you are bold enough to tell me lies about your whereabouts,' said the general.

The captain looked at the lieutenant who would not meet his gaze.

"I know about the unchristian games you played all day yesterday on a holy first day of Christmas,' said the general. 'We will hold a trial and make sure justice is done.'

A trial was held, and the general ruled that this lack of discipline would not be tolerated. The captain was sentenced to death by firing squad.

They stood the captain on a small hill and gave him one final wish. He asked if he could have one last meeting with his beloved. It was denied. He gave a necklace to the lieutenant asking him to give it to Hilda. Then he cried out, 'I love you Hilda!'

The soldiers covered the captain's head with a black sack, they loaded their weapons, aimed and fired at the captain.

The soldiers left Hylte and marched towards Skåne.

On their way they passed Annerstad where the villagers lined the streets waving to the Danish soldiers as their priest had asked. Hilda couldn't see her captain but spotted his friend, the lieutenant. She ran to him and asked where her captain was. He handed her the necklace and filled with shame at his cowardice he said, 'He has no use for it, where he is now.' The lieutenant shook his head. In the midst of those crowds of smiling, waving citizens of Annerstad, Hilda's face crumpled and tears sprung from her eyes as her heart shattered.

Her father came to her 'What is it? Where is he?'

'He is no more father', and she sobbed uncontrollably in his arms.

The next day, some of the Swedes who had been hiding in the forest, came out as it was now safe for them to move around. They found the body of the Danish Captain on the hill in front of Hylte farm. They carried the body into Angelstad. They were met by Hilda and her father, the priest of Annerstad, who suggested to them that he was buried right next to the church wall.

The Danish Captain's execution had shaken the two villages. Whatever they had felt about him before, they all thought the cruelty of the Danish general was brutal and unjustified. A funeral service was held in the church and it was full of people from Angelstad and also people from Annerstad were attending.

Peace eventually came to Småland and everyone celebrated, but the Danish Captain was never forgotten.

15

KING CHRISTIAN IV AND JENS LONGKNIFE

Jens Langkniv, as he was called in Denmark, is our Robin Hood, stealing from the rich and giving to the poor. The truth might be that Jens was nothing like Robin Hood, but as some storytellers say, 'Never let truth stand in the way of a good story'.

There was a time when King Christian IV was young, vital and indestructible. He loved to hunt and before a big hunt it was tradition for the king and his men to gather for a wild night of drinking. The party only ended when eight servants peeled the enormous king's body from the wine-soaked table and carried him up to bed. The morning after, while his huntsmen were staggering from their chambers with splitting headaches, Christian would be fresh and wide awake, sitting proudly in his saddle, waiting for his suffering companions to join him. When the horn sounded and the hunt commenced, King Christian rode wilder and faster than any of his men.

Well, that was before. Before wild arrogance and self-glorification led him to believe he was the prophesied 'Lion of the North' who would defeat the 'Eagle from the South'. He led Denmark into battle against the Holy Roman Emperor's army in Barenberg, Germany, certain of victory, only to find he was no lion but in fact a frightened puppy who could by no means match the great armies of the south. He scampered back to Denmark, tail between his legs, and one year later the Holy Roman Emperor's army invaded Jutland. The land was occupied for two long years until a peace treaty was eventually signed. But war had ruined King Christian and his kingdom, and when this story begins Christian IV was a shadow of his former self.

It was morning in Viborg in the middle of a now liberated Jutland. The old King Christian had slept well after a sober night and was sitting in his saddle eagerly awaiting a great hunt. His hosts, the noble men of Viborg, saluted him, and the dogs were barking. It was to be the first hunt with the King of Denmark since Jutland had been liberated from the German Catholic occupation some years before. This was Christian's chance to prove that despite defeat on the battlefield he could still handle a rifle and bring down a stag.

By late afternoon the men were all tired. They had caught nothing and were ready to call it a day and return to the estate. But the king had a ferocity about him, and a desire to prove he still possessed the spirit of his youth, so he kept riding onwards alone, into gentle valleys covered with juniper bushes, past still blue lakes, and then across brown, unbroken heathland and down towards the boggy woodlands. He spotted a stag and he stopped. He saw it disappear into the muddy forest and for one moment King Christian hesitated at the sight of this uninviting black swamp covered with silver birch trees. But then he spotted the deer again a little further into the forest. He edged forward into the woods, raised his rifle and shot. The deer fell forward and a cry of victory came from the king's mouth. He blew his horn.

The horns answering him were far away to the east, on the safe heath ground. Then he spotted the wounded deer again rising to its feet, then limping its way into the fog that was hovering over the watery marshland.

As the king followed the deer into the mist, suddenly a silhouette of a man appeared before him.

It was one of the tallest men Christian had ever seen. He suddenly felt the cold from the mist, or was it the fear that came into his body?

Christian stopped his horse and reached for his sword. Pointing it at the man, he slowly moved forward.

He could see the man's eyes were dark and his feet were bare. His coarse clothes, which had once been white wool, were stained with dirt and blood.

Then the king noticed a knife hanging in a sheath strapped to the man's hips. The knife had a rope attached to it and suddenly Christian knew who it was he had in front of him. It was Jens Longknife, the murderous criminal that had been stealing and killing for the past twenty years around the forests of Midjutland. And here he was, standing right in front of the king and looking like he wasn't afraid at all. Christian reached down and found his horn. He blew it.

'I know what you are trying to do,' said the tall dark man with a little smile on his face. 'You know who I am and you think you can call your men here. They will not be able to find their way into these woods, as you will not be able to find your way out without my help. Before this day there were only two who knew how to come here, and now one is dead.' Jens nodded towards the body of the deer.

A distant blast of a horn sounded far, far away. He had to get out of there. Christian didn't believe Jens, he was the king and of course he could find his way out of this muddy, watery dark place. He turned his horse around and then it stumbled into a watery hole. He cursed, dismounted and helped the horse out, but once more the horse slipped and fell into an even bigger waterhole. Using all his might Christian pulled the horse out and back onto safe ground.

'What do you want from me to get me out of here?' said Christian.

'Not much,' said Jens, 'and you can be certain that I will not hurt Your Majesty. I'll show you the way out of here and for that I just need a small favour.'

'What is that?' said Christian.

'My mother was burned at the stake some years ago. She was accused of being a witch,' said Jens. 'Can you change it so she in her death is honoured for who she was?'

'Who was she?' said Christian.

'My mother was the kindest, most gentle, caring woman you could ever imagine. She was an angel, not a witch,' said Jens.

'Why did they call her a witch then?' said Christian.

'To get to me,' said Jens. 'Instead of catching me out in the forests, they punished me by taking my mother and burning her. She doesn't have a grave in the graveyard, no blessing from a priest.'

'I promise you, I will make certain that we will find her records and if your mother was not a witch we will let it be known in the church,' said Christian.

'I believe you,' said Jens. 'My mother deserves to be in heaven.'

They heard the sound from the king's fellow huntsmen, now a little closer.

'When we meet your hunting friends, they will come after me,' said Jens.

'I will make sure they will let you go for this day. But I can't promise you anything tomorrow,' said the king.

'Nobody can!' said Jens and he disappeared from the king's view.

Moments later Jens appeared in front of Christian's horse, grabbed the rope and led it out of the forest. It was getting dark and Christian was happy to have a guide. He could feel the coldness from the water surrounding him, he could hear the howls of the wolves and the splashing of his horse's hooves when they stepped outside the thin line of solid ground that led them out of the swampy hell.

He heard the blast of his fellow huntsmen's horns and he was reaching for his horn when Jens turned around and shook his head.

'Not yet,' he said. 'Wait till we are out on solid ground.'

When they arrived on the heath, they could hear the horns coming closer and Christian blew his in response. They heard the barking of the dogs getting louder.

Jens said goodbye to the king, turned around and the tall dark man disappeared into the dark forest. At the same moment Christian spotted the first torch from his fellow huntsmen.

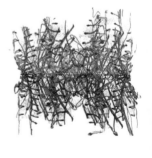

16

PRINCE VILDERING AND MISERI MØ

When I discovered that there is a famous children's book in the UK called *Misery Moo* I did a lot of research trying to come up with another word for this powerful woman. I gave up. She is Miseri Mø and the name suits her well. The Danish word 'Mø' means virgin or maiden and Miseri doesn't really mean anything in Danish, but it could be related to the English word 'misery'.

Once upon a time a king was out hunting in a forest with all
his knights.

> In the green forest the hunting men
> deer and hare caught in deepest glen

The king had the fastest horse and after a while he found himself
alone. Suddenly a thick fog made it hard for the king to see where
he was leading the horse. He was riding in a bog and the horse was
struggling to find tussocks to tread upon and suddenly it slipped
and its front leg fell into the water. The king used all his power to
lift the horse back onto the tuft of grass it had fallen from. A little
further on the horse slipped again and its back legs disappeared
into the swamp. Again the king saved his horse, but the third time
it was the whole horse that started sinking and the king barely
managed to stay on solid ground while the horse was swallowed
up by the deep dark waters.

As he tried to find his way out of the fog, the king had to hop
from tussock to tussock, sometimes slipping into the water and
pulling himself back onto the ground.

Suddenly he saw a little man standing on a tuft calmly looking
at him. He had a beard going all the way down to the ground and
a wooden stick in his hand.

'Please,' said the king, 'Can you help me? I will give everything
if you can get me out of these waters.'

'Yes,' said the little man, 'you are in deep trouble. I am the only
one that can help you, and you will surely die here if I don't, but
in return for my help I need one thing from you. The first male
that is born in your castle when you return home must be given
to me when I come to collect it.'

The king thought about his queen, who was carrying his child.
'It could be a girl,' he thought. And in the castle there was also a
pregnant cat and cow and dog all ready to give birth. Even chicks
in the yard would probably hatch before his own child was born.
Besides there was nothing else that would get him home and the

sun was setting fast now. He knew he may not survive a night out there in the bog. So he agreed.

'Here,' said the little man and threw his stick to the king, who was so taken by surprise that he didn't catch it, but the stick didn't seem to care and it started walking from tuft to tuft like it knew exactly where to go.

'You'd better be moving. Just follow the stick and it will take you home,' said the little man.

The king followed the stick out of the swamp, into the forest and finally all the way up to his castle. Then the stick turned around and went back into the forest.

When the king stepped inside the castle, he heard a scream from his wife and then the cries of a newborn baby. When he walked into the queen's room and saw her holding a baby boy in her arms, he was heartbroken. When the queen heard what her husband had done and that the little man would come and collect his reward any day, they agreed that the queen should find a way to buy some time.

They called their son Prince Vildering and when he was only two weeks old, the little man came for his reward. He stood next to the queen, who was sitting by the prince's bed.

'He is mine, you know,' said the little man, 'the king gave me his word and a king's word cannot be broken.' The queen agreed, but asked the little man if he could just give them five years to be with their little son. She offered him 100 of their best oxes if he would do that. The little man nodded in agreement and said, 'Five years and I'll return.'

Prince Vildering grew up in the castle and he was a kind and good boy. When he was five years old the little man came again. The queen again bought them another five years with 200 oxes.

When the boy was ten years old the little man came again and the queen bought another five years with 300 oxes. This time he said, 'I have enough cattle now. Next time I want my reward. After five more years it will be fifteen years since I helped the king out of the boggy waters. When the boy is fifteen, he is mine.'

In that last five years Prince Vildering learned how to fight, to ride a horse and many other things useful for a prince to know. He was a handsome, strong, clever and well-behaved prince in all matters.

On his fifteenth birthday it didn't matter how many oxes the queen offered.

'A king's word has to be trusted,' the little man said. 'I will let my stick be here and tomorrow it will show the prince where to go. And if he doesn't come, I will let this castle be swallowed by seven feet of boggy waters and everybody in it will drown.'

Next morning Vildering said goodbye to his sobbing parents. He took the stick and started walking away from the castle towards the forest. Once they were outside the castle the stick flew in between the prince's legs and lifted him up into the air. He didn't know if he was riding or flying; as fast as the wind he was carried over hills and valleys, forests and fields, rivers and lakes, until in the evening he felt ground under his feet again and the stick in his hand. He stood in front of a castle dug into a hill. Outside the castle the little man with his long beard and round eyes was waiting for him.

'Good evening, troll,' said Prince Vildering.

'Here I am called king or master,' said the little man, who was in fact a troll. 'And I would like to strangle you right away, just to teach you not to be so bold in your mouth. And I will right now if you can't tell me three pure truths with no lies hidden within them.'

'I can give you three truths with no lies within,' said Prince Vildering. 'Never have I lain more softly than in my mother's womb, never have I tasted sweeter than from my mother's breast, never have I brought her more sorrow than on this day.'

The troll softened. 'I can hear that you are well trained, but here you can learn more. Tonight is free time for you. Take a look at everything and tomorrow you will see that you have to work to live here.'

Inside the castle was lots of gold and silver, but Vildering was used to that, so he didn't take much notice. He walked past a room where twelve sleeping giants, all servants of the troll, lay. Then a room with a bed where an ugly woman with a nose as long as herself was sleeping. Her servant was a young woman, fair and sweet, who looked up at Vildering and they both smiled.

Next morning Vildering was woken up by the troll, who shouted that he had to eat his breakfast fast. Vildering sat down and the young woman served him delicious porridge.

The troll came in and said, 'Come with me, I will show you what you shall do to earn your dinner.' And the troll took Vildering out to a forest and said, 'Here is an axe,' and pointed at a long-handled axe that Vildering could hardly lift. 'Chop down all the trees in the forest before I return for the evening. If you haven't chopped down every single tree before evening, you shall die.'

And then the troll left Vildering to do his work. He swung the axe into one of the trees but it hardly made a mark. He tried another tree with the same result. He must have tried to cut a hundred trees but he couldn't chop down one. He was sitting on the ground with his head in his hands when the young woman came with his lunch.

'Here you are,' she said and gave him some bread and meat. 'Why aren't you busy chopping and why are you so sad?'

'I am going to die tonight because I can't chop down this forest as the troll told me to,' said Vildering. 'That is why I am sad, wouldn't you be?'

'I think I would,' said the young woman, 'but let me help you cut down the trees so you don't have to be so sad.'

'Could you do that for me?' said Vildering.

'If I help you, you will let me down one day,' said the young woman.

'No never,' said Vildering. 'If you would help me, I would be yours for ever. What is your name, young woman?'

'Miseri Mø,' said the young woman. 'I was born a princess, and I was kidnapped like you some years ago, but I have learned a few things from the troll and his mother in my time here.'

The two of them talked and laughed. They liked each other straight away. She told him that she was supposed to be scratching the head of the old mother of the troll but she had wanted to bring him lunch so Miseri Mø had made the cat do the scratching and the hag never felt the difference. The cat would get some cream in the evening, so he never told anyone about this.

Vildering laughed some more, but he felt bad for Miseri. She was such a bright young woman who had been forced to be a slave to such horrible characters. Vildering told her about the castle where he was born and she told him about the things that she had learned and that Vildering could trust her. It would only take a minute to cut down that forest.

And so late in the afternoon Miseri Mø stood up, held her apron in front of her, waving it, and said:

Chop the trees, trees lay down
Flatten the forest to the ground

The trees fell down one by one and soon all the trees in the forest lay on the ground.

So when the troll came in the evening, he saw that the job had been done. All the trees in the forest were cut and lying in log piles.

'Did you do that all by yourself?' the troll asked Vildering.

'Yes of course,' said Vildering. 'There was no one here to help me.'

'Well,' said the troll, 'if there was one, that one wasn't born yesterday. Go and get something to eat.'

And so Vildering had another meal at the troll's house cooked and served by Miseri Mø.

Next morning the troll took Vildering out to a sheep path, nearly one mile long and piled high with sheep dung. 'Clear the dung from the path. Use the shovel and just throw it to the sides of the path. It hasn't been cleaned for a hundred years so there is some work ahead of you. If you can't do it before the evening comes, you are going to lose your life tonight.' And the troll was gone.

Vildering could hardly lift the shovel it was so heavy and he tried his best to clear the dung but the piles were so high that after hours of shovelling he had barely scratched the surface. He threw down his shovel and began to cry. And that was how Miseri Mø found him when she came to serve his lunch.

'What is wrong with you today?' she said.

'Today it is even worse,' said Vildering. 'The troll told me to clean this path piled high with one hundred years of sheep dung. And if I can't clean it before evening, I will lose my life.'

'If I help you, you will let me down one day,' Miseri Mø said quietly.

'No,' Vildering said, 'I would never do that.'

'Very well,' she said, 'let us sit down and have our lunch and talk.'

And so they sat and talked and found that the company of the other was very pleasant.

Late in the afternoon Miseri Mø stood up and said:

Dung, go with shovel, shovel, fling dung
This is no work for a king's son

When the troll came back that evening, the path was cleaner and shinier than it had ever been.

'Did you do this yourself?' said the troll.

'Yes of course,' said Vildering. 'There was no one here to help me.'

'Well,' said the troll, 'if there was one, that one wasn't born yesterday. Go and get something to eat.'

Next morning the troll took Vildering out to the stable.

'There you will find Vrinsker,' said the troll. 'Vrinsker is a grey stallion and he is a good horse but he is thirsty. Ride Vrinsker to the lake and let him drink. And if you can't, you shall die tonight.' And the troll left Vildering outside the stable.

As Vildering stepped inside the stable he saw a grey stallion tied with an iron chain with seven locks to hold him. When the horse heard Vildering it began neighing wildly and hammering his hooves to the ground, kicking up sparks as it did so. The horse bared his teeth with an angry grin and fire came blasting out of his nostrils as it tried to kick Vildering with its hind legs. Vildering barely escaped the horse's fury and ran out of the stable.

When Miseri Mø came with his lunch, Vildering was sitting outside the stable, head in hands, crying.

'If I help you, one day you will let me down,' said Miseri Mø.

'No, I will never!' Vildering said.

'This is the hardest of the tasks the troll has given you,' said Miseri Mø.

She took a handful of hay and stepped inside the stable:

Still now still dear stallion grey
Here, eat your fill of corn and hay

And Miseri Mø moved softly toward the stallion and it calmed and ate from her hand.

Gently she whispered:

Vrinsker, Vrinsker, gentle stallion grey
Carry Prince Vildering on his way

She blew on the seven locks on the chain and immediately they opened.

She gave Vildering hay and told him to give it to Vrinsker. The stallion calmly ate from Vildering's hand and soon Vildering had climbed onto the horse and was riding down to the lake, where the horse drank the sweet, cool water. He led the horse back into the stable, Miseri Mø blew and locked the seven locks and went back to the castle to scratch the hair of the troll's mother.

The troll came and saw that the horse was well and he asked again, 'Did you do this all by yourself?'

'Yes of course,' said Vildering. 'There was no one here to help me.'

'Well,' said the troll, 'if there was one, that one wasn't born yesterday. Go and get something to eat.'

Later that evening Miseri Mø heard the troll and his mother talk.

'Miseri Mø is getting too clever,' said the troll. 'She has fooled me three times now and it is time for us to get rid of her. Let us eat them both together tonight.'

'Uhm,' said the troll's mother, 'I have long been thinking about how that princess will taste and now I am going to have a double meal, you are a good boy after all!'

The troll called Miseri Mø and Vildering in and told them to start the oven for cooking something very large.

'Stoke the fire well,' said the troll. 'We need it extra hot tonight.'

Then the troll and his mother had a sleep before dinner.

'We need to run tonight,' said Miseri Mø to Vildering. 'That hot oven is for you and me.'

She told two pieces of wood to answer back when the troll asked if the oven was hot enough. Miseri Mø and Vildering walked out into the stable, where Vrinsker was waiting for them. She unlocked the seven locks with a blow, and they sat up and galloped out of the courtyard away from the troll and his mother.

The troll woke up after a while and called out, 'Is the oven warm enough now?'

'Not yet!' said the log with the voice of Miseri Mø.

The troll slept some more, woke up and called out, 'It must be warm enough now!'

'Not yet!' said the other log with the voice of Vildering.

The troll slept some more, woke up and called out: 'It surely must be warm enough now!'

When there was no answer the troll stood up and found that it had been the logs answering and that Miseri Mø, Vildering and the horse Vrinsker were gone. He called for his twelve giants and they flew after them as fast as they could.

Miseri Mø held the mane of the horse and Vildering had his arms around Miseri Mø as Vrinsker was galloping as fast as the wind.

But after a while Vrinsker spoke, 'There is sweat on my back.'

Miseri Mø told Vildering to look behind.

'The troll's giants are coming after us and it looks like they are flying in the air,' said Vildering.

Miseri Mø stopped the horse and said:

A bush you'll be, a stone will he
I a flower for the giants to see

When the twelve giants passed by they stopped for a second to smell the pretty flower and then rushed on. When they realised that they had lost track of the three runaways, they turned around and came back to the troll.

'They just vanished into thin air,' the giants said with shame.

'Did you see anything?' said the troll.

'We saw a rosebush with a sweet-smelling red rose and a stone next to it,' said the giants.

'That was them, you fools,' said the troll and hurried out after to catch them himself.

As he galloped onward, Vrinsker said, 'There is sweat on my back.'

Miseri Mø told Vildering to look behind.

'The troll is coming and he is coming fast,' said Vildering.

Miseri Mø said:

A church you will be, its yard will he
I a priest for the troll to see

The troll looked at the church for a moment and snarled at the priest, but then he continued the pursuit. After a while he realised they were gone and he returned to his house, where his mother was waiting for him.

'Suddenly they were gone,' the troll said.

'Did you see anything?' said his mother.

'I saw a church, a graveyard and a priest in front of the church,' said the troll.

'That was them, you fool,' said the troll's mother and hurried out to catch them herself.

As he galloped onward, Vrinsker said, 'There is sweat on my back.'

Miseri Mø told Vildering to look behind.

'The troll's mother is coming after us and she is coming fast,' said Vildering.

'She is the cleverest of them all,' said Miseri Mø. 'That is going to be the hardest.'

A drake you will be, a lake will he
I a duck for mother troll to see

When the troll's mother saw the two ducks swimming in the lake, she called them, shouting, 'Rap rap rap, come and have your bread,' but the ducks ignored her. So the troll's mother took a troll apple with a string attached to it from her pocket. She threw it at the two ducks, and had the apple hit any one of them the troll mother could have pulled them back. But the duck dived in the water, taking the drake with her before the apple could harm them. Then the duck flew up out of the lake and bit the string so the apple fell to the bottom of the lake. With that, all the mother troll's magic was gone. She flew into such a rage that she turned to flint and then shattered into a great shower of tiny flintstones that spread across the fields. That was the end of the troll's mother.

Miseri Mø, Prince Vildering and Vrinsker became themselves once more and they rode calmly further on until they came to the kingdom of Prince Vildering's father.

Miseri Mø changed the horse to a stone they could sit on. She said, 'You think you have only been gone for a short while. It is not so. It is seven years ago you left the castle. And your mother is dead. Your father is still alive and he has found another wife who has a daughter. Your father and his new wife have a little son together. When you come into the castle, tell your father everything and then come and get me here by this stone. But don't let anyone kiss you. If you let anyone kiss you, you will forget all about me.'

Vildering promised not to let anyone kiss him inside the castle, and told her how much he loved her and how thankful he was for everything she had done for him. He gave Miseri Mø a kiss and went in to tell his father everything that had happened to him.

Inside the castle he was greeted by his father and his father's new wife carrying a little baby boy, Vildering's half-brother. She wanted to kiss him, but he just shook her hand, then she insisted that he should give his half-brother a kiss, but he just embraced him. Then a greyhound came running to say hello to Vildering. He thought it was his old dog and let him lick his face with its tongue. At that moment Vildering forgot all about Miseri Mø. He had no memory of what had happened in the house of the troll, so when the king asked him where he'd been, he said it was all gone from his memory.

'No wonder,' the king said, 'you have been betrolled.'

The greyhound ran out of the room and a moment after, the daughter of the king's new wife entered the room. There was much joy and celebration of the prince's return. The daughter of the king's new wife danced with Vildering and he was enchanted by her charm as they danced into the night.

Outside the castle Miseri Mø understood what had happened. She made the stone into a little calf and went around the castle to find the kitchen entrance, where she told the servants that she was without a father or a mother and that she only owned this little calf and asked if it is was possible to get some work at the castle.

'You can be our hen girl,' said one of the servants. 'You shall take care of the hens, give them food and water and gather the eggs every morning. There is a little house next to the henhouse where you can sleep and you will find room for the calf.'

Miseri Mø moved into the little house and did her work. She didn't see Vildering and he had forgotten all about her. He was engaged to the daughter of the king's new wife and they were going to be married very soon.

The servants in the castle started talking about the new hen girl, she was so beautiful and clever and could do all kinds of work. She could sew a stitch straighter than had ever been seen before in the castle.

At the castle everybody was getting ready for the big wedding celebration. The king's personal servant had seen Miseri Mø and decided to ask her to make him a shirt, though it wasn't really a shirt that he wanted. She said that it was easily done and he could take the shirt away with him the same evening. So he came down one evening and sat on a chair waiting for Miseri Mø to make him a wonderful shirt.

And so she said:

Scissors, cut linen, needles, sew cloth
make a shirt he will never take off

When the shirt was finished the king's servant didn't leave. He said that he didn't mind that she was just a plain hen girl and he was the king's most trusted servant, they could be lovers anyway. Miseri Mø just smiled and asked him if he could do a favour for her. If he could be so kind as to shovel the ash from the fire because the shovel was too heavy for her. So the king's servant stepped into the fireplace, and the moment he took the shovel Miseri Mø said:

Shovel, work with this man through the night
toss ash in the bucket till the morning light

In the morning the king's servant was covered in ash from top to toe and he was exhausted. He crept back to the castle ashamed. When the other servants asked him how it had been down in the hen girl's house, he showed them the fine shirt and smiled like it had been the most wonderful night.

Then the king's footman thought he would try his luck and he went to Miseri Mø to ask for a fine shirt. Miseri Mø just smiled sweetly and said:

Scissors, cut linen, needles, sew cloth
make a shirt he will never take off

When the shirt was finished the king's footman didn't leave, but tried his best to kiss her, but Miseri Mø avoided his advances and asked him if he could do her a favour. If he could be so kind as to go out to the henhouse and put the pin in the iron hook to lock the door. When the footman came to the henhouse door Miseri Mø said:

Pin, work with this man throughout the night
keep locking the door till the morning light

The footman stood the whole night trying to place the pin in the iron hook. In the morning there were many holes in the door from the many missed attempts. He quietly crept into the castle.

He also boasted about the fine shirt and said nothing about the hard times he had had standing outside in the night closing the henhouse.

Then the king's marksman tried. He also came and asked for a
shirt. Miseri Mø said:

Scissors, cut linen, needles, sew cloth
make a shirt he will never take off

When he tried his luck Miseri Mø asked him if he would be
kind enough to bring the calf in for the night. She watched him
approach the calf and take it by the tail when she said:

Calf, you must run far into the night
The man will chase you till morning light

And the calf made the marksman run over the hills, down through
the valleys, through the forest, across stony land and marsh land,
the whole night he ran. In the morning he was totally exhausted
but there was no time to rest, because this day was the wedding
day for Prince Vildering and his bride.

The carriage with Prince Vildering, his bride and a little following of trusted men were making their way out of the castle on
their way to the church when the shaft of their carriage broke.
When they replaced it with a new one, that broke immediately
too. So the king's personal servant said that the hen girl in the
little house close to the castle had a solid shovel that could replace
the shaft. When they asked Miseri Mø if she would lend them her
shovel, she said, 'My mother wasn't known to be asked by servants
and I am no less than my mother.' So Prince Vildering had to ask
her. He couldn't recognise her, but she was very kind to him and
gave him her shovel. It was perfect for a shaft and so they drove
on towards the church.

A little further down the road, one of the hubs holding the
wheels fell off. When they replaced it with a new one, it broke.
So the king's footman said that the hen girl also had a pin that could
hold the wheel. Again Prince Vildering had to ask. She was very

kind to him and gave him the pin from the door of the henhouse. Still he didn't know who she was. And the carriage carried on.

Right in front of the hen girl's house the carriage fell into the ditch. And it was impossible for the six horses to get it out of the water. So the marksman suggested they ask the hen girl if they could borrow her calf. Prince Vildering went to her for the third time and again she was very kind. The calf pulled the carriage out of the water and ran all the way up to the church in a blink of an eye and they were married.

On their way back, they left the calf by the hen girl's house, and replaced it with the six horses.

Prince Vildering said to one of the servants that he should go and invite the hen girl to the wedding party that night. She had been helping them and it would be a token of his appreciation to let her be at the wedding. Miseri Mø said that she would be happy to be part of the wedding celebration at the castle.

When Miseri Mø entered the great hall of celebration there was a moment of silence. None of the guests could recognise the hen girl; her dress was embroidered with every flower of the forest in silver and gold threads. In her hair she wore a crown of flowers that made her look like a queen, and when she smiled, it was like the sun bursting into the wedding hall. On her shoulders were two birds, a dove and a cock. She sat down right in front of the wedded couple. She took three grains of barley and threw them on the table. The cock flew down and took two of them and left one for the dove and when the dove had eaten it the cock pushed the dove so it fell off the table and Miseri Mø said:

You shun your love, and throw her away
As Vildering does to Miseri Mø this day

The birds flew back to the shoulders of Miseri Mø. Prince Vildering thought he recognised the name Miseri Mø, but he couldn't work

out from where. Miseri Mø took six grains of barley and threw
them on the table. The cock flew down and took four of them
and left two for the dove and again he pushed the dove off the
table. Miseri Mø said:

Now you let down the one that helped you before
Like the Prince swept Miseri Mø to the floor

The birds returned to the shoulders of Miseri Mø. Prince
Vildering was getting more and more insecure. Who was this
wonderful woman and why was she talking about him?

Miseri Mø took nine grains of barley and threw them on the
table. The cock flew down and took six of them and left three for
the dove and for the third time the cock pushed the dove off the
table and Miseri Mø said:

Now you let down, she that helped you to sing
As Miseri Mø was by Prince Vildering
She waited for him on a big grey stone
Now she lives in the henhouse all alone

The birds returned to the shoulders of Miseri Mø. Vildering
jumped up from his seat. He suddenly remembered everything.
It was like a curtain in front of his eyes had lifted and he could see
clearly for the first time in a long time. He looked at Miseri Mø
with eyes filled with love and looked confused at his new bride.
He spoke to all the guests at the wedding, 'Once a beautiful casket
was made for me to keep my beloved belongings in and for it I
had a gold key made. Then I lost the gold key and I got a silver
key in its place. Now I have found the gold key again and now I
ask you all, what is your advice to me? Shall I use the gold key or
the silver key?'

They all agreed that he should use the gold key. Prince Vildering
continued, 'As you all give me that advice you have to forgive me
that I have to push my bride away and marry the princess that

is sitting there with two birds on her shoulders. She alone is my dearest, as I owe her everything even though I had forgotten all she had done for me when I returned home to the castle.'

Now Prince Vildering remembered everything and he told the whole story from the beginning, all the way to the moment when he stepped into the castle. Then Miseri Mø said, 'I told you not to kiss anyone because then you would forget me. And you did not kiss your stepmother, even when she asked for a kiss, and you did not kiss your half-brother, even if your stepmother wanted you to kiss him. But you let the dog, the white greyhound kiss you, and that white greyhound is none other than the bride that is sitting next to you today.'

Then they all understood that the queen was a witch and that she and her daughter had betrolled the prince. The king immediately put the queen, her daughter and their little son in a carriage that drove them back to the country where they had come from. And now there was a real wedding for Prince Vildering and Miseri Mø.

In the evening just before bedtime Miseri Mø said, 'Will you be kind and fetch the little grey calf that lives in my house and bring it up to the castle? That calf was Vrinsker, the horse who helped us escape the troll. Let it be locked inside a bedroom where the bed is made for a man to sleep in. Also place in that room some new clothes that will fit you.'

When that was done, the bride said to her husband, 'Now you shall be mine and I shall be yours and I will have nothing just for me. I have within me all the magic I learned from the troll and his mother. I must be free from that. You shall place a cauldron with cold water next to the bed and when you see me getting into bed tonight, push me into that cauldron, so I will be covered in cold water. When you then lift me up, all my magic will be gone.'

He did what she had told him, and when they were in the bed together, he said, 'I am a little sad that you don't have your magic any more. It saved us many times.' She just smiled a smile that he couldn't really figure out.

In the morning they went to the guest chamber and there they found a prince that looked like Miseri Mø the way that only a brother can look like a sister. He was in fact her brother that the troll had betrolled and he was a human now because there was no longer a Miseri Mø. Miseri Mø was gone and instead there was now the woman who was married to Prince Vildering and soon to be Queen Miseri.

17

THE DEVIL'S
COFFEE GRINDER

I dedicate this story to Nanna from our food club. She was our neighbour for many years and she always asked me to tell this story of why the water in the ocean is salty.

Once there were two brothers who lived close to each other. As time passed one brother had become rich and the other brother had not such good fortune. The rich brother built his house on top of and the poor brother built his cottage at the foot of the same hill.

It was one Christmas evening when the poor brother in his cottage was looking at the food spread upon the table and he thought to himself, 'This is the biggest celebration of the year, but this is not a Christmas dinner!'

His wife had done everything she could to make it look Christmassy. But two eggs and some dry bread simply wouldn't pass for a Christmas dinner, however many candles and twigs from fir trees you placed around them.

Where was the duck, the brown sugar potatoes, the red cabbage, the thick brown sauce, the red wine? It wasn't in the poor brother's house. They both knew that at this same moment his rich brother would be making the final preparations for a Christmas dinner with all the traditional dishes and a little bit more on top of that. And with this thought, the poor brother told his wife to wait for him and left the house.

He walked up the hill to the rich brother's farm, where he could smell the roast duck, the roast pork with the crispy fat around it, the hot sugar potatoes and the red cabbage. In the kitchen there were pots everywhere, the ovens were filled with delicious food and the poor brother just stood there, his mouth watering, looking at it all.

The rich brother came in a hurry.

The poor brother said: 'Glædelig Jul!'

The rich brother was a little bit unsure what was going on and looked at his brother suspiciously. The little brother surely hadn't gone all the way up the hill just to say 'Glædelig Jul.'

'Glædelig Jul to you as well, dear brother,' said the rich brother, 'and no, I have nothing to spare.'

'My wife said that you would say no,' said the poor brother, 'even if I told you we only have two chicken eggs for our Christmas dinner. But I didn't agree with my wife. I said that you will give your brother something of a good heart on this Christmas eve.'

'What kind of nonsense is that?' said the rich brother, 'I don't *have to* give you anything. But I suppose if I refuse to give you food on this sacred evening your wife will tell the story to all her friends. Here!' The rich brother threw a pork rib (in Danish: flæskeside) to the poor brother and said, 'Take this and go to hell!'

The poor brother thanked his richer brother and left the farm.

Outside he thought that the best way to look for hell on a Christmas evening was down in the churchyard. So he went there and looked around. In the churchyard he saw a tall man in a black coat digging a grave. It was like his eyes were glowing in the night and he appeared to float above the ground.

'Excuse me,' said the poor brother, 'do you know where I can find hell?'

The man didn't speak. He just stopped digging for a while and pointed down into the grave. So the poor brother jumped into that deep grave. The poor brother fell down down down through the air of the deepest hole and landed softly in the middle of hell.

He saw a big group of devils come running towards him literally screaming their heads off. They placed their heads back on their shoulders and reached out towards the poor brother and especially what he was holding in his hands. 'Give it us! Give it us!' they screamed and shouted as they were stamping on the ground. Like all devils they loved the taste of pork. Pigs all over the world are eager to go down to hell and meet their friends, the devils. Just take a look at a pig, they have their big round noses deep in the ground while they are saying 'hronk, hronk, hronk' meaning 'devil friend, here I come.'

The poor brother held on to his pork rib and suddenly the Master Devil stepped forward and made all the other devils step back.

'What is this?' said the Devil.

'It is pork, sir,' said one of the smaller devils.

'I can see that,' said the Master Devil, 'and you want some pork, do you?'

All the small devils jumped up and down, screaming.

'And you wanted to steal it from this fine young man?' said the Master Devil.

The smaller devils all nodded wildly.

'We can ask him nicely,' said the Master Devil. 'Maybe he will give it to us.'

'I am sorry,' said the poor brother, 'but we have no meat in our house, and this is our Christmas dinner.'

The smaller devils all started shouting, 'Steal it, steal it!'

The Master Devil shouted, '*Be quiet!* Look, this is what is wrong with you and why we have such a bad reputation on the earth, let us be sensible and offer this fine man something in return for the pork meat.'

One of the small devils ran away and came back with a coffee grinder.

When the poor brother was offered a coffee grinder he said, 'What shall I do with a coffee grinder? We have no coffee and we need some food, not coffee.'

'But this is not an ordinary coffee grinder,' said the Master Devil, 'this is the Devil's coffee grinder so it can make everything. You whisper into the grinder and tell it to make some potatoes, there you have your potatoes. And here is what you say to make it stop again.'

And the Devil whispered into the poor brother's ear what to say to stop it doing what it was doing. The poor brother handed over the pork rib and the devils started a big fight over who was going to have which part.

The poor brother went home and entered the cottage, where his wife was waiting patiently. When she saw what he brought with him, she gasped and said, 'Why did your brother give you a coffee grinder? He knows that we don't have any coffee, that is just to insult you.'

The poor brother said, 'Please wait and see.'

And so he placed the coffee grinder on the table and asked for a roast duck, and in that moment a roast duck appeared on the table. He asked for roast pork with the crispy crackling fat around it, then some hot sugar potatoes and nice sweet/sour red cabbage, some nice plates, red wine and two wine glasses. The grinder did all that he asked, and when there was enough food for Christmas, he whispered the words to make the grinder stop.

While they sat down eating and drinking the wonderful delicious meal the poor brother's wife, full of love for her husband and gratitude to the Devil, said, 'let us invite our neighbours for lunch on the second day of Christmas. Now we have our coffee grinder to make everything, we can treat our neighbours to a good Danish Christmas lunch.'

And so the next day the poor brother and his wife walked around the neighbourhood with invitations made by the coffee grinder saying, 'Come home to our house for a lovely second day of Christmas, lots of food and drinks. Bring your instruments!'

When the rich brother saw what was happening, he was confused.

'What are they going to serve for all these people?' the rich brother thought to himself. 'A single pork rib?'

On the second day of Christmas he went down to the poor brother's cottage and to his surprise there was all the food for a good Danish julefrokost: herring, leverpostej, cucumber in vinegar, chicken, meatballs and cheese, lots of different kinds of cheese, Danbo and the blue one. And a big barrel of beer. Singing and laughter filled the room.

The rich brother went over to his brother and said, 'Where did you steal all this food and all that beer? Two days ago you had nothing.'

The poor brother showed him the coffee grinder and told the rich brother that he could ask it to create whatever he wanted. And so he asked the coffee grinder to make a roasted chicken and some wine. The rich brother stared at this magical machine producing a delicious chicken and some wine to go with it. The rich brother thought about what the grinder could do on his farm.

'I want that grinder,' he shouted. 'How much?'

'Do you want to buy our grinder?' said the poor brother.

'Yes,' said the rich brother.

'Well,' said the poor brother, 'thirty kroner, but I will not give it to you before autumn, I need it here for me and my wife during spring and summer.'

'Good,' said the rich brother, 'here is thirty kroner and you bring it up to my farm the first day we harvest the fields.'

The poor brother promised that, and the rich brother left the party and they all joined the joyful singing and dancing.

The not-so-poor brother and his wife did well during spring and summer. They just asked the Devil's coffee grinder what they wanted and in the same moment, it was there. When harvest time came, they lived in a bigger house and they wished for enough gold to keep them well for the rest of their days.

The first harvest day, the poor brother took the coffee grinder and went up to the farm of the rich brother. All the rich brother's staff were out harvesting the fields, so when the not-so-poor-any-more brother stood there with the coffee grinder the rich brother said, 'Well, you kept your word, good for you! Put the grinder in the kitchen, I will make lunch today.'

When it was time to prepare for lunch, the rich brother told the kitchen staff that he would prepare the food. And he went into the kitchen, took the grinder and wished for porridge and herring, something they hadn't had for a long time.

And so the grinder started making porridge and herring. The rich brother filled the biggest pot with porridge and herring, then he filled a bucket with porridge and herring, then he filled a large bathtub with porridge and herring, and then he realised that he had not been told how to stop this grinder from doing what it was told to do.

When the staff came home for lunch they found the rich brother in the kitchen with porridge and herring all over the floor and the rich brother desperately trying to stop the grinder making more porridge and herring, but the grinder would not stop and the kitchen became so full of porridge and herring that the window collapsed and porridge and herring poured out into the courtyard.

The rich brother gave up. He just sat there looking at the river of porridge and herring in the courtyard moving slowly down towards the not-so-poor-any-more brother's house.

When the not-so-poor-any-more brother saw the river of porridge and herring flowing down towards his house, he put on his rubber boots and waded through the river to the rich brother's house to ask if there was anything he could do.

'Make it stop, please!' said the rich brother.

'I will,' said the not-so-poor-any-more brother, 'but then I will take the grinder with me.'

'Yes,' said the rich brother, 'take it away from this farm.'

The not-so-poor-any-more brother made his way into the kitchen where the grinder was floating on the surface of the porridge and herring busily making more porridge and herring. The not-so-poor-any-more brother said the words to make it stop. And the grinder stopped.

Once back home in his house, he said to his wife: 'Let us make a golden house and find a good place by the sea with a nice view.'

'I would love that,' said his wife. And they asked the grinder to make a wonderful golden house and placed it on top of a hill with a beautiful view of the ocean.

There was a captain sailing by on his ship bringing salt from the salt mines in Norway down to Denmark. He just loved that new golden house and he admired it every time he passed by. So one day he anchored his ship and had his men row him ashore. He walked up to the golden house, where the not-so-poor-any-more brother sat enjoying the view with his wife.

'How come you can afford such a fantastic house?' said the captain.

'It is because we have a coffee grinder that makes us everything we want,' said the not-so-poor-any-more brother.

The captain thought about how tired he was sailing back and forth, Norway to Denmark, every day the same.

'How much for that coffee grinder?' asked the captain.

'Thirty kroner,' said the man.

And so the captain handed over the sum and took the grinder. 'I just talk to it and it will make me everything?' said the captain. The man and his wife just nodded.

So the captain went on board his ship and told his men to sail back to Denmark. They didn't have to go up to Norway, he would fill the ship with salt from the grinder. And so in the middle of the North Sea/Vesterhavet he asked the coffee grinder to make salt and he filled the ship and then he realised that there was something that he had forgotten. He didn't know how to make it stop. And so when the ship was filled to the brim with salt and the ship was about to sink, one of his men shouted to the captain, 'Throw the salt grinder in the ocean!'

And so he did. He threw the Devil's coffee grinder overboard, and saw it sink still making salt. And that is why the ocean is salty. Because the grinder is still making salt and it will do so until someone knows the words to make it stop.

18

THE DEVIL AND THE BLACKSMITH

Is the Devil inside or outside ourselves? Sometimes I hear the stories from these people telling them a long, long time ago and I understand that they knew more than we know now.

Once there was a blacksmith who had made a deal with the Devil that the Devil would make him as comfortable as could be for fifty years, but in return the Devil could take the black-smith on his fiftieth birthday. And so it was that the blacksmith had a good life with enough work to keep him busy and there was always plenty of food, wine and money in his house.

One day three riders stopped by the blacksmith. It was the Lord himself, Jesus Christ and St Peter. Among the three it was always St Peter who talked to the people they met. 'Please, Mr Blacksmith,' said St Peter. 'Can you take a look at the horse of the Lord? The shoe fell off when we came into the valley here. We had all three horses shoed when we left paradise, but you know how it is, all the good blacksmiths are not with us up in heaven, rather they are all down in hell with the Devil and his people. We will reward you according to the quality of the shoemaking.'

'Certainly, St Peter,' said the blacksmith. 'Please find yourself a comfortable place to sit in the shadow of the pear tree and I will bring some juice from the pears. Most delicious if I may say so myself.'

And so God, Jesus and St Peter sat and watched how this very skilful blacksmith shoed the white horse of the Lord. When he had shoed one foot, he asked if he should remove the rest and replace them with some good solid shoes instead of the flimsy ones the smith up in heaven had made. The three men, or they weren't really men, but you know what I mean, nodded, and so it was that the Lord himself sat on a white horse with four freshly made, high-quality horseshoes. St Peter thanked the blacksmith and said he had done an excellent job on the Lord's horse. 'I will grant you three wishes for your good work.'

'Well,' said the blacksmith, 'My first wish concerns the three-legged stool in the middle of my workshop.'

The blacksmith pointed at the stool and St Peter nodded, he had already noticed the stool. 'I want everybody who sits on the stool to stick to it, unable to move until I say that they can go,' said the blacksmith.

'A strange wish,' said God to St Peter. 'It is like he does not care about what happens to him after life. The blacksmith should wish for eternal salvation after death.'

'My second wish,' said the blacksmith, 'is about the pear tree you have been sitting under. There are a lot of boys climbing into that tree and stealing my pears. I want everybody who climbs up into the pear tree to be stuck in the branches until I say that they can climb down.'

St Peter said that the wish was granted. 'Once again he forgot to wish for his salvation,' said Jesus Christ.

'Finally my third wish,' said the blacksmith. St Peter, Jesus and God listened with wide-open eyes expecting the blacksmith to use this last wish for eternal afterlife in heaven. Instead the blacksmith took out an old tattered purse from his pocket.

'I hate it when my wife or my men steal a shilling or a krone from my purse. Make it so whatever is put inside my purse can only leave it with my consent.'

'You have your three wishes,' said St Peter and mounted his horse. The three men left the blacksmith and God looked down on his horse's hooves and gave a little nod of approval.

On the morning of his fiftieth birthday the blacksmith went inside his workshop and found that the Devil was waiting for him.

'Now, go and collect your tools,' said the Devil. 'We have a long walk ahead of us.'

'I understand,' said the blacksmith. 'Please sit on the stool there and wait for me, I won't be a minute.'

The Devil sat on the three-legged stool and heard how the blacksmith called to all his men that they should bring all their tools. The Devil was stuck on the stool while the blacksmith and his men used their hammers, crowbars and other tools to beat the Devil. The Devil screamed, 'What shall it take to stop you beating me?'

'Ten more years,' said the blacksmith with a big smile. He was granted ten more years and the Devil was released from the stool. He left the workshop. Behind him he could hear the blacksmith and his men celebrating ten more years of a good life for the blacksmith.

On his sixtieth birthday the Devil was waiting for him in the garden. It was a wonderful, warm late summer's day and the pears in the tree were at their best. Juicy, soft, tasty, oh, it was a treat to eat pears from that tree. All the boys in the village had stopped plundering the tree after the first year when they found themselves stuck in its branches. So this year the tree hung heavy with fruit. The blacksmith gathered his tools and when he came out of his workshop the Devil was standing under the pear tree admiring the pears.

'They look delicious,' the Devil said. 'I would love to taste one.'

'Yes,' said the blacksmith. 'I could climb up into the tree and pick some pears for our journey.'

'No,' said the Devil, 'I am not stupid, you will play a trick on me once you're up in that tree. I will climb up there myself. Then you can wait under the tree and collect the pears when I throw them down to you.'

And so the Devil climbed up into the tree and picked the two most juicy pears and was just about to throw them down to the blacksmith, but he was nowhere to be seen. The blacksmith had left the garden and was calling all the boys that used to steal his pears.

'I think there is a thief in my pear tree boys,' said the blacksmith. 'Hit him with a stone.'

And so the boys threw stones at the Devil, who couldn't defend himself.

'Ouch,' said the Devil, 'When I come down from this tree, I will teach you a lesson, ouch!'

The boys stopped their happy game of stone throwing, but the blacksmith told them that there was nothing to be afraid of because the Devil wasn't able to climb down that tree any more than the boys were ten years ago.

The Devil cried out, 'What do you want?' and another stone hit him.

'Ouch,' said the Devil. 'Please don't hit me! I will give you anything.'

'Ten more years and no revenge on the boys,' said the blacksmith.

'Yes, yes, you have ten more years and I won't hurt your boys, I promise.'

The Devil climbed down the tree and went back to hell.

The blacksmith climbed up into the tree and picked a great basketful of pears. The blacksmith shared the pears among the boys and the men from the workshop and they sat in the sunshine with pear juice dripping down their faces.

On his seventieth birthday the blacksmith began to feel his age. He enjoyed the quietness of a Sunday afternoon tea with his wife and maybe one friend more than the excitement of daily life in the workshop. But still he thought that there were some more years left in him to enjoy this world, so when the Devil came to collect him, he made sure that he had his purse with him. The Devil was suspicious of the blacksmith, so there would be no sitting on stools or climbing trees.

They walked along the road away from the village. As they walked past a giant poplar tree the blacksmith stopped and admired it. He said, 'Is it true that you can transform yourself into whatever you like?'

'Yes,' said the Devil, 'I can do that. Everything I want to be, I can become.'

'So you can be as tall as that tree?' asked the blacksmith.

And there was a devilish sound and then the Devil became taller than the tree. 'Impressive,' said the blacksmith, and took the purse out from his pocket.

'Can you make yourself so little that you fit into this purse?' said the blacksmith.

And whooooshh, the devil was inside the purse. The blacksmith closed the purse and suddenly he was very deaf. He couldn't hear the sound from the desperate Devil trying to escape from the purse.

The blacksmith returned to his workshop and told all the men working there once again to bring their hammers. The Devil shouted from inside the purse that they should not beat him.

The sound of the Devil was thin and weak, but the blacksmith knew what he was saying, so the blacksmith told the Devil that they would start hitting the purse with their hammers if the Devil didn't do what he wanted. With his tiny voice the Devil said that he would do anything the blacksmith wanted as long as the blacksmith just released him from his tiny prison. The blacksmith asked for ten more years, which he was granted. The blacksmith released the Devil and he ran back into hell wishing never to see the blacksmith again.

Now the blacksmith was old and he was ready to go. So he died one lovely spring day. He was buried with his tools, as they were back then. He walked all the way up to St Peter and found St Peter outside the gates of heaven checking if the right people were entering paradise. St Peter looked bewildered when he saw who it was that wanted to enter.

'So it is you,' St Peter said. 'What do you want here? You had your chance to choose one of the wishes to be your eternal salvation. You didn't, and I think you have a friend down in the other department. I think the Devil will be very pleased to invite you into hell. So bye for now.'

St Peter turned around and told a priest that just because he was a priest he wasn't automatically granted heavenly admittance. That depended on how he had served as a priest. The blacksmith didn't bother to hear the priest's answer to that, so he turned around and found his way down to hell.

He knocked on the door and it was the Devil himself that opened the gate to hell.

When the Devil saw who it was, he gave a scream and said that the blacksmith under no circumstances was allowed entrance to hell.

'But St Peter up in heaven won't have me, and he said that you were my friend and I have to be somewhere, so I thought I could just as well be here in hell.'

'I won't allow it,' said the Devil. 'You are just going to make a lot of trouble. Now leave.'

The Devil wanted to close the door, but the blacksmith was quicker than the Devil. So he threw his bag of tools in the doorway and it wouldn't close. The Devil screamed and ran away. The blacksmith sat down beside his tools thinking of what to do next.

And if you have ever wondered why the gate to hell is always open, now you know.

19

THE DEVIL'S BEST HUNTER

This little section of Devil stories continues with a story of a soldier being ninety-nine years, thirteen months and three days old. It makes no sense and that is sometimes the beauty of these old stories, that the logic lies in the rhythm and the repetition of the words. Try saying the phrase with different energy and speed. It changes the story if you say ninety-nine years, thirteen months and three days angrily, softly, slow, fast etc.

A soldier had served his country and his king for ninety-nine years, thirteen months and three days. Yes, it was ninety-nine years, thirteen months and three days that the soldier had spent in the army of his country. A long time, if you ask me. He was tired of the routines that he knew so well and wanted to see what life could offer him outside the camp.

He went to his sergeant, a brutal little man with an enormous belly and small evil piggy eyes.

'What do you want?' barked the sergeant when he saw the soldier approaching.

'I do not want to be a soldier any more,' said the soldier, 'I would like to seek my fortune in real life, outside this army camp, with normal people.'

The sergeant burst into a horrible, cruel laughter. 'You think you will find your fortune out there in the real world,' said the sergeant. 'You are useless as a soldier even though it is all you know of in life. So how do you think it will be in the real world without me and the lieutenant to take care of you? I guarantee you, you will return within a month begging us to take you back.'

'Maybe that is true,' said the soldier. 'Nevertheless, I would like to have my money for serving my country for ninety-nine years, thirteen months and three days.'

'I do not have your money,' said the sergeant. 'Go and ask the lieutenant.'

The sergeant was kind compared with the lieutenant, who was a tall, thin man with no sense of humour. He enjoyed punishing the soldier by hitting him in the neck with two fingers. His grey eyes looked coldly at the soldier.

'What?' snapped the lieutenant when he heard that the soldier wanted to leave the army. 'You are so stupid and useless, you will never survive out there.'

'That may be so,' said the soldier, 'but I will give it a try. And please let me have my money for serving in the army for ninety-nine years, thirteen months and three days.'

The lieutenant threw three shillings on the ground in front of the soldier, who picked them up shaking his head. Three shillings wasn't a lot of money, not even then. The soldier packed his things and walked out of the gate of the army camp with a smile on his face and three shillings in his pocket. Once out of the gate he didn't look back, not even a glance.

The soldier found himself in a marketplace with lots of people. The soldier had spent ninety-nine years, thirteen months and three days looking at the sergeant's ugly face and being slapped by the lieutenant's two fingers. So the soldier walked around the marketplace with a happy smile on his face looking at all the different kinds of people.

His three shillings didn't last long though. So the soldier knew he had to find a job of some kind. He asked the people selling stuff from their tents if there was anything he could do for them for a small payment. Suddenly the soldier felt a strong hand squeezing his shoulder.

'I hear you are looking for some work,' said the stranger. He was a tall dark man with a deep, strong voice. His dark blue velvet coat covered him from the neck to the feet and his eyes were glowing. If the soldier could have seen under that coat, he would have seen that the stranger had a hoof for a foot. We know what that means, but the soldier wasn't aware of any danger.

'I have a job for you,' said the stranger, 'and I pay good money. A bag of pure gold if you serve me well for a year and a day.'

'Sounds good to me,' said the soldier, and followed the stranger out of the marketplace, into town.

Once in town the stranger went into an empty alley, where there in the darkness stood a house. They went inside, and in the kitchen there were three tall man-sized pots full of boiling water. Under each of the three pots burned a fire.

'You only have to take care of the fires and I will be your master,' said the stranger to the soldier. 'That is all I ask of you. Make sure that the water is boiling all the time. And don't worry about filling them with water. There will be plenty of water all year round. And most important of all, do not look inside the pots. Whatever happens to the pots, do not lift the lid to take a look. Work well and I will reward you well.'

The master left the soldier to take care of the fire under each of the three pots.

It went well for three months. Then one day the fire under the first pot stopped burning. When the water had stopped boiling, the soldier heard a strange sound from within the pot. It was the sound of an angry man. The soldier couldn't help himself. He lifted the lid and peeked inside the pot.

Much to his surprise, the face of the ugly sergeant was staring at him shouting, 'You useless idiot, get me out of here before I cut you into pieces.'

The soldier put the lid back on and started the fire again. After a while the only sound in the kitchen was the fire crackling under the three pots and the boiling, bubbling water.

It went well for another three months. Then one day the fire under the second pot stopped burning. When the water had stopped boiling, the soldier heard the sound of the lieutenant shouting from within the pot. The soldier lifted the lid and peeked inside it. Sure enough, there was the lieutenant's face staring at him, shouting that the soldier should get him out of there. The soldier put the lid back on the pot. After a while the crackling fire and the bubbling water were again the only sounds.

Three months passed. The fire under the third pot stopped burning. When the water had stopped boiling, the soldier heard nothing. He lifted the lid and peeked inside the pot. There was a sound of somebody running fast into the kitchen. Although the soldier couldn't see him, he felt the presence of his master running towards him. The shadow slammed the lid back on the third pot and vanished out of the door as fast as he came in. Then only the sounds of fire crackling and water bubbling and boiling were to be heard in the kitchen.

When the year and a day had passed the master returned, gave the soldier a bag full of gold and asked him if he wanted a job that could earn him three more bags of gold. The soldier nodded. He would love to have all that gold.

Then suddenly the master ran forward, grabbed the soldier by the neck, opened the third pot and threw the soldier into the boiling water. The master then dragged the soldier out of the water, placed him on a table and pulled the boiled skin off his body. Then he ripped the soldier's skeleton of all its muscles. He found some fresh, new muscles and put them on the soldier's old bones, found skin, eyes and hair of a young man and put it on the body of the old soldier. When the soldier opened up his eyes he was a young version of himself, and this young man stretched his body and felt the strength of youth once again. He looked into a mirror. A transformed man looked back at him. It was a young man in all his power. And a handsome young man if you ask me.

The master took a light brown sheepskin coat that covered the young man's body from top to toe. 'Wear this brown coat for three years without taking it off,' said the master, 'and in the three years to come you will not have a wash. When people ask you anything, just tell them that you are "the Devil's best hunter".'

So to make sure that the young man had everything he needed the master gave him a magic purse. A purse that would never be empty, but always full of gold. The master also gave the young man a deck of cards. 'Play with these cards and you will always win,' said the master.

The young man now calling himself 'the Devil's best hunter' went around in the kingdom for three years without a wash and without taking the sheepskin coat off for all that time.

After three years of telling everyone interested that he was the Devil's best hunter he was on his way back to the house in the dark alley.

On his way he came to a lovely inn lying next to the road. When the Devil's best hunter entered the inn, the innkeeper stared at him with disgust. And when the Devil's best hunter asked for the best room, the owner just laughed and told him to sleep in the barn with the other animals.

'The best room with the best view is reserved for the king. Tonight he is still out in the forest hunting and when he comes back, he needs that room. And as I said you can sleep in the barn. You are too filthy to be sleeping in my inn.'

The Devil's best hunter didn't say anything to that, instead he just started piling up gold on the counter. When the counter was covered in gold, the owner stammered and said that he could make an exception this one time. The Devil's best hunter was installed in the king's chamber.

The king returned from the hunt frustrated and angry. Not a deer, not a wild boar, not even a single rabbit was the result of a whole day's hunting in the forest. When he heard that his room was occupied by the Devil's best hunter, he started shouting that it was his room and how could the innkeeper do this to a king and didn't he know the consequences of his act?

The innkeeper showed the king how much gold he had been given for just one night.

'Does this hunter really have that much gold?' asked the king.

'Yes,' said the innkeeper, 'he has a purse and that purse is just full of gold.'

'Bring him to me!' said the king.

And so the filthy, horrible-smelling Devil's best hunter was brought to the king.

'Are you a hunter?' said the king.

'I am,' said the Devil's best hunter.

'Well, it is too late to go hunting now,' said the king, 'but tomorrow morning I would like you to join us even though you smell really bad. And I hope you understand that I need my room with the view. I always sleep in that room when I am here.'

The Devil's best hunter said, 'Well I can't just give it to you, but we can play for it in a game of cards!'

The innkeeper gave them a deck of cards and they sat down to play a game of Mousel, an old Danish game, that is all about luck. The king won the first game, winning the right to sleep in the room with the view. Thrilled with his win the king cried, 'Let's play again!'

The Devil's best hunter agreed to another game but his oily, dirty hands had made the cards stick together so the innkeeper gave them a second deck of cards to play with. The king won again. They played game after game every time with a fresh deck of cards from the innkeeper and every time the king won gold from the Devil's best hunter's purse. He was ordering many drinks and he was sitting there laughing and having the time of his life.

Finally the innkeeper said, 'I have no more cards for you, you've ruined every single deck I own.'

'Well then,' said the Devil's best hunter. 'Let us play with my cards.'

And he produced a clean bright deck from his pocket. 'These cards will never get dirty no matter how many games you play with them.'

And so the game commenced with the Devil's best hunter's cards and then the king's good fortune changed. The king lost. He lost everything he had won, and then he lost more. His castle, his livestock, his land, everything until there was nothing left to put at stake.

So the Devil's best hunter arranged to go with the king to the castle to collect his winnings. The king was devastated at having lost his entire kingdom and the Devil's best hunter could see it, so he asked the king if he had any daughters.

'Yes I have three,' said the king.

'Then if one of them will have me,' said the Devil's best hunter, 'I will allow you to live in the castle for the rest of your life.'

It was the best the king could hope for so he agreed to give one of his daughters away, that was if one of them would accept a marriage with the Devil's best hunter.

As the carriage came to the door of the castle, the princesses came running to greet their father. Out of the carriage stepped a stinking hairy monster. It was the Devil's best hunter, who was now the owner of everything in and around the castle. The princesses gave a scream of disgust and ran back towards the castle. Then they heard their father calling them back.

The king had stepped out of the carriage too and he told them what had happened to him. Their father explained he had lost everything in a game of cards and that he would now have to live on the street like a beggar. The only way to avoid this fate was if one of the princesses would marry his companion.

'I know it is much to ask from you,' the king said, 'but if one of you will marry this man, I can stay in the castle.'

The two oldest sisters gave a scream of disgust and ran into the castle, crying that they would never lower themselves to marry a stinking monster. They would rather throw themselves in the ocean. The youngest daughter just looked at her father and said, 'If that is what has to be done to let you stay here in your beloved castle and not live out on the street, I will marry this man even though I find him appalling.'

When the king and the youngest daughter went inside the castle, the Devil's best hunter welcomed them. He was the owner and could do what he wanted with the castle and everything that was in it.

On his way out the Devil's best hunter talked to the youngest daughter.

'Do you like me?' he said.

'No,' she said, 'I do not like you, I find you disgusting, but I would rather suffer with you than see my father on the street begging for food.'

'Very well,' said the Devil's best hunter, 'I will leave you now to make ready for our wedding.'

He broke a ring in two halves and gave one half to the princess. 'Take this half ring. When I come back, I will be changed and you won't recognise me. But ask for the other half of the ring and you will know it is me. I will leave you now and in three days we will marry.'

Then he rode back to the Devil. The master was waiting for him. 'You have served me well, so here are three bags of gold as I promised. And there is a bath ready for you. When you get married, you'd better make sure you look like a noble man.'

And so the Devil's best hunter went into the bathroom and found a hot bath, a razor, fine new clothes and some sweet-smelling oil. When he came out of the bathroom, the master nodded in approval and said, 'You are most certainly a very handsome man and now you are also a rich man. The princess is going to be proud of you. But you need a carriage suited for your outfit and some horses.'

He went and found a bucket with six eggs. He went outside with the Devil's best hunter. The master threw one egg on the ground and with a thunderous noise the egg became a white horse. He threw another and another and with a clap of thunder each one of them became a beautiful white stallion. The master then threw the basket down hard on the ground and it became a golden carriage. The Devil's best hunter climbed aboard the carriage and was ready to leave. He nodded to his master as the six white horses set off and in that moment he suddenly saw the hoof under his master's coat. He glared into the eyes of the Devil before him. The Devil just smiled and said, 'Good luck, you handsome prince.'

The youngest princess stood at the castle gate waiting to see an ugly-looking, bad-smelling, animal-like creature that she then should marry. Instead, a young handsome prince riding a fine carriage with six white stallions entered the castle's courtyard. The young prince stepped down from the carriage and told the servants that he was going to marry one of the princesses in the castle and that the castle belonged to him. The youngest princess ran up to this prince. From a little purse she took out half a ring and asked for the other half. The prince smiled and gave her the other half. The two halves matched perfectly and the youngest princess gave a cry of joy, kissed the prince and told him that everything was ready for their wedding.

When the two eldest daughters realised how foolishly they had behaved they jumped into the moat surrounding the castle and drowned themselves.

The Devil made a simple calculation. He had lost one soul, but he had gained two souls, in the two eldest daughters of the king.

20

THE MERMAID THAT LAUGHED THREE TIMES

This mermaid story is like no other mermaid story I know of. And so is the mermaid that Tea created to illustrate the story. I was blown away when I met Tea's mermaid for the first time and it still makes me laugh.

Once there was a man who drove out to the sea to collect some sand. Then a mermaid came up to him and said, 'If I can come with you and stay in your house for three years, I will pay you well.' He said yes and took her with him.

When they arrived at the man's house, his wife was not happy but the man told her they would be rewarded so the woman put the mermaid to work. She gave her a spinning wheel and told her to spin some yarn. There the mermaid sat spinning at the spinning wheel, but the mermaid was the slowest spinner that the woman had ever seen.

On Sunday the man and the woman invited the mermaid to attend church with them, but this would be the first and only time that they invited her, for in the church in the middle of the priest's sermon the mermaid burst into such loud laughter that she could be heard far far away. They were so embarrassed that they kept the mermaid at home from that day on, sitting at the spinning wheel spinning ever so slowly.

Time passed and the tax collector was coming and the man looked very worried. He said to his wife, 'What am I to do? I have no money.' Again the mermaid laughed that loud laugh that could be heard far far away. 'What is wrong with her?' the wife said. 'How dare she laugh at us when all she does is sit there spinning ever so slowly and eating all our fish.'

'Don't worry, I am sure she will pay us as she promised,' the man said.

When the three years had passed and it was time for the mermaid to leave, the woman was happy as she was fed up with the mermaid. She hadn't spun enough yarn to earn her keep and she wanted her gone. The mermaid asked to be driven back to the place where the man had found her three years earlier, and so he did. When she climbed out of the carriage, the man was standing waiting for her to reward him. Instead she began to laugh again. That same loud laugh that could be heard far away.

'Why are you laughing?' said the man, now a little worried.

'I am laughing at your wife who has been so angry with me for sitting by the spinning wheel for three years complaining about how little yarn I have spun, and today as I left, she angrily cut away the three years' worth of yarn I had spun and threw it in the corner. If she had looked more carefully she would have seen that I was spinning gold.' The man looked shocked.

'Lucky for your wife she was so angry that she did not take it all off the spinning wheel,' she said. 'There is still one little thread left and that is of pure gold. She can make dresses and golden blankets from that little thread, it will never end. But all she cut off is of no use now.'

Then the man grew curious and asked, 'Tell me, what were you laughing about when I sat at the table and cried because I did not have money for the taxes?'

'Well,' she said, 'there was a pot under your feet full of money. You could have taken that if you had wanted, and you can still go home and find it under the kitchen floorboards.'

The man looked happy.

'But tell me why you were laughing when we went to the church together?' he asked.

'Yes, that was funny,' she said, 'because the Devil himself was sitting behind the priest writing down the names of all the people who were sleeping while the priest was giving his sermon. The Devil had a calfskin stretched out to write upon, but it soon filled up and there was not enough skin for all the names and so he wanted to stretch it to make it even wider. He took the skin between his teeth and held it with his hands. Then suddenly his teeth slipped and his head hit the pillar behind him. He looked so stupid that I couldn't help it, I just had to laugh.'

The man thanked the mermaid and watched as she swam out to sea.

He went home and found the pot with money under the kitchen floor, and his wife had all the gold she wanted on her spinning wheel.

21

THE SHOEMAKER'S
BOY

Sometimes these stories surprise you in the best way possible.
I wasn't expecting that Spain would suddenly appear in the story.
And it just makes me laugh and I want to find out more.

Once there was a son of a priest and he
was meant to be studying to be a priest
like his father, but both of his parents
died when he was very young and so a
shoemaker took care of the boy.

The shoemaker gave him regular
beatings and so the boy soon
learned how to measure, cut,
make holes in the leather with
an awl, thread a needle and sew
a shoe together, but the boy never
cared about all that knowledge. Often he sat in
deep thought instead of threading the needle,
or he was looking up at the sky instead of
hammering pegs into the leather.

One day the shoemaker told the boy to go out into the forest and cut some elderberry branches for pegs. So the boy went into the forest, where he soon forgot about pegs. He listened to the birds, enjoyed watching the squirrels as they ran up and down the tree trunks gathering food and he went down to the lake and saw how the sun reflected in the water. The boy felt at home in the forest and it was a long time before he remembered why he was there, so then he started looking for an elderberry tree. When he had found one and started cutting branches, he heard a voice and when he turned around he saw a grey dog who spoke to him, 'Please, can you help us? We are trying to figure out a way to split a deer among us, so each of us will be happy. There is a brown bear, a white falcon and a black ant and me of course, the grey dog.'

'I can try, please show me the way to the deer,' said the shoemaker's boy.

He followed the dog deeper into the forest, where he found the dead deer lying on the ground next to a tree. In the tree a white falcon was squawking, the bear walked around in circles growling and the ant was shouting up in the tree. The boy asked them to be quiet.

He said, 'the best way to split a deer among you would be to give the head to the ant, as the head is filled with holes for you to crawl around in, the intestine should be for the falcon, soft and delicate for your beak, the bones with meat on is for your grey dog to gnaw upon and the body for the bear as you are big and strong.'

'I would love the skin of the deer if it is not too much to ask for,' he said. The animals were pleased with that way of dividing the deer and agreed to give the skin to the boy. The shoemaker's boy took out his knife and peeled off the skin of the deer. He was certain that the shoemaker would be pleased with such lovely skin and maybe then the shoemaker would give him less of a beating.

As the boy walked through the forest, he heard the dog running after him, barking and calling. 'Please, can you come back, the bear wants to talk to you?'

The boy thought that the bear had regretted that he had taken the skin of the deer, and he was scared as he followed the dog back to the animals.

The bear was very gentle and told him that they all wanted to thank him for his clever advice. And for that they all wanted to give him something more.

The bear told him that the boy was now gifted with the power to become a bear just as strong and clever as him. The dog said to the boy that whenever he wanted he could become a dog who could run like the wind and smell what's coming 100 miles away. The white falcon said that the boy now had the power to be a falcon like him, with beautiful feathers, swift wings and sharp eyes. And finally the ant said that the boy could be just as tiny, as pretty and wise as she was.

The ant said, 'You can be all of us and then when you wish, you can be yourself again.'

The boy thanked them and walked towards the shoemaker's shop. He thought about how the shoemaker would treat him after a whole day in the forest dreaming. There would be a lot of beating waiting for the boy.

'Why not try to be a falcon?' he thought to himself. 'I am now a falcon,' he said loudly and a moment later he found himself flying over the treetops and he could see further than ever before. There was nothing for him to come back to the shoemaker for, so he started flying south, until he reached Spain.

The white falcon spent the day flying around looking at people and places. Everything was strange and colourful. When the sun was about to set he spotted a peculiar castle. As the white falcon came closer and circled around the castle he saw that all the shutters were closed on the windows to the east, south and west and only the windows to the north let the light in.

The castle belonged to the king of Spain and his daughter. The queen had died many years ago when the princess was just a little baby. Her father loved his only daughter more than anything. It was for her sake that the castle was built the way it was. It had been predicted at the princess's birth that if the sun shone on her before she was thirty, she would immediately be taken by a troll. She was now fifteen and only in the evening after the sun had set could she walk in the garden. Her maids were there walking with her and her father. The falcon saw it all and waited.

When the princess was left alone by the window of her room, the falcon landed in a tree close to the window and the princess raised her head. She had recently lost her blue parrot and the parrot's cage was still hanging in the tree with some of the food scattered on the floor of the cage. The princess saw how the white falcon cautiously flew into the cage and started picking up some of the corn left behind by the parrot. The princess slipped out into the garden. When she was so close that she could reach out and grab the cage, the white falcon looked at the princess for a short moment and then continued the picking of corn. The princess closed the door to the cage, shutting the falcon inside, and carried it into her room and hung it on a hook attached to a rope hanging down from the ceiling. The princess gave the falcon some more corn and talked gently. The falcon stopped picking and listened to her soft gentle voice.

'It is so nice to have you here,' she said. 'I am getting lonely here in my room without any sunshine. I can't be out in the sun for another fifteen years as my mother was forced to promise a troll that the moment a sunbeam hits me I am to be with him.'

She opened the cage, let the falcon land on her arm and stroked the bird gently.

In the night, as the princess slept in her bed, the falcon became an ant and the ant slipped out of the cage and when the ant became the shoemaker boy the princess woke up. Distressed by the sight of a young man in her bedroom, she screamed with fear and her servants came rushing in. When they searched the room there was no young man to be seen. In the cage was the white falcon.

In the morning the princess took the cage with the white falcon to the window. She placed the cage next to her and looked out into the garden. Then the falcon spoke to her.

'I am so sorry I frightened you in the night.'

The princess looked amazed.

'You can talk,' she said.

'I can do more than that,' said the falcon. He told her about the four animals that he could change into and that he was the young man the princess had seen in the night.

'Show me,' said the princess.

The ant made her laugh, she liked the dog, she feared the bear and when she saw the young man that she had seen before in her room she smiled and asked him for his story. He told her everything.

She told him how she longed to see the sun and how she had heard people talk about her beautiful country she had never seen in daylight. There was so much to talk about and the two of them loved to be together.

When the servants came to serve lunch the white falcon was back in the cage.

One day the Spanish princess told the shoemaker's boy that she would like to marry him but her father would never accept a poor shoemaker's boy that could become a bear or a dog when he wanted it. She gave him a bag of money and said that he should buy fine clothes, beautiful horses and some servants. Then he should return and tell the king that he was a prince from Denmark and wanted to marry his daughter.

When the servants came in that afternoon, the cage was empty and the princess sat by the window looking happy. The servants didn't know what to think. The princess seemed to be so enchanted by the white falcon, but now that it was gone, she looked even more happy.

Not long after, a fine knight came riding into the courtyard telling the king that he was Prince Falcon from Denmark and that he wanted to marry his daughter. The king looked at the handsome prince and all his servants.

'It will be my pleasure to let you have my daughter, but are you aware of the spell? The princess is not allowed out into the sun before she is thirty years old, and that is fifteen years from now. If she is exposed to a sunbeam, the troll will have her for the rest of her life.'

'I shall take care of your daughter,' said Prince Falcon.

The wedding lasted for a week and a day. The celebration spread to one of the neighbouring castles where a tournament with music and dance was to be held. Prince Falcon could see that the princess wanted to go and witness the spectacle for herself so he went outside and had a look at the sky. He came back and convinced his wife that there would be no sunshine on a grey day like this. And so they went to the neighbour's garden. When they stepped out of the carriage the clouds parted for a second, but it was enough, and a single sunbeam hit her.

A gust of wind took the princess and Prince Falcon was left alone.

He transformed himself into the grey dog, which began following the scent of the princess. It took him into the desert till it ended by a mountain. The dog was sure she was inside that mountain. The ant found a little hole in the mountain and crawled in. Inside was the Spanish princess sitting on a sofa where an ugly troll was lying half asleep. The princess combed his ugly hair.

The ant crawled up and whispered that it was him, her beloved. She smiled and stopped combing.

'Why do you stop, stupid princess?' asked the troll.

The ant told her to ask questions to the troll.

'I was wondering,' said the princess, 'where do you come from?'

'What kind of foolishness is this? Comb my hair, woman, that is what you get your food for. If you have to know, I come from nowhere and everywhere, which is the same.'

She continued combing his ugly hair and the troll was grunting happily.

The ant crawled up to the princess's ear and encouraged her to ask more questions.

'You are strong, troll, but is there anything you are afraid of?' asked the princess and she stopped combing the troll's hair.

The troll shouted, 'Comb my hair, you fool. And stop all this talking, right away. Don't ask more questions or I will kill you and eat you for my dinner. I am not afraid at all. What could it be that could frighten me?'

'I don't know,' she said, 'but I am afraid to lose my heart to a handsome prince.'

'I can never lose my heart and I can never die because they can't find my heart,' the troll said.

She combed his hair and the troll was happy for a moment.

The ant crawled up to the princess's ear and encouraged her to ask more questions.

'Where is your heart?' she said and stopped combing.

The troll jumped up. 'I am tired of you stopping combing my hair. Tonight I am going to eat you and you better prepare for that, you fool.'

'I am sad about that,' she said. 'And as I am going to die soon, it won't hurt you to tell me where your heart is.'

'If I didn't know better I would have thought that you had a man listening to all this nonsense. But there is no man and there is no one to rescue you, my dearest princess of Spain. So it is safe to tell you the secret of my heart. My heart is hidden in an egg and the egg is in a duck, and the duck is in a hare and the hare is in a dragon and the dragon is in a lake far away in a land called Poland. Now comb or I will eat you right now.' And so the princess combed the troll's hair.

The ant crept out of the mountain and the white falcon flew to Poland looking for the lake.

By a lake he saw a farmer leading twelve fat pigs down towards the banks. The falcon flew down and became the prince and he asked the farmer why he was leading the twelve fat pigs down towards the lake. The farmer stopped on top of a hill looking down at the lake.

'It is sad,' said the farmer, 'but there is a dragon in the lake and every day we have to give it twelve pigs or we will be eaten ourselves. Soon there will be no more pigs in our country and then we won't know what to do.'

'Wait here,' said the prince.

The farmer saw how the prince went down towards the bank of the lake and called out over the water. When the dragon came stomping up from the lake to have his lunch of twelve pigs, the prince was gone. Instead the dragon met a bear, strong and mighty, who fought the dragon, but they were equally strong and there was no winner to be found. After a long, exhausting fight the dragon said, 'If I only had the meat of the twelve pigs in my belly, I would win over you.'

And the bear replied, 'If I only had some wine and some bread, I would win.'

Both the bear and the dragon abandoned the fight and the dragon turned with a roar and disappeared into the lake.

The farmer with his twelve pigs was delighted that the dragon didn't get the pigs today and when the prince came walking from the banks of the lake, the farmer took him home and gave him a bed to sleep in for the night.

Next day the farmer took twenty-four fat pigs down towards the lake. The prince asked him to wait on the hill and walked ahead. When the dragon crept up from the water it was met by the bear. After a long fight the dragon said, 'If I only had the meat of the pigs in me, I would win over you.'

And the bear replied, 'If I only had some wine and bread, I would win over you.' The dragon turned around and disappeared into the lake.

In the evening the farmer sat in the inn and talked about the bear that had fought the dragon for two days in a row and said that he had heard the bear saying something about wine and bread.

'The dragon is starving and the bear wants wine and bread to win,' he said, and the men laughed.

The son of the innkeeper heard the story and next day he followed the two men down to the lake. The farmer had thirty-six fat pigs with him and the prince once more disappeared down by the lake. The bear and the dragon were fighting as usual but it was clear that the dragon was hungry and soon it said, 'If I only had the meat of the pigs in me, I would win over you.'

When the bear replied, 'If I only had wine and bread, I would win over you,' the innkeeper's son jumped forward and gave wine and bread to the bear.

The bear had his wine and bread and after the meal he had gained his strength and killed the dragon. Out from the dragon jumped a hare, fast as lightning. The bear became a greyhound that caught and killed the hare on a hill. Flying out from the hare, a duck tried to escape and the hound became a white falcon. The falcon caught the duck in the air, killed it and out from the duck came an egg that landed on a stone without a crack.

The falcon became the prince and he looked at the unbroken egg. He knew where to break it, where there was something harder than this stone.

He went back to the banks of the lake where the farmer and the innkeeper's son waited for him. The prince told the innkeeper's son how brave he had been throwing the bread and the wine to the bear in the middle of the fight. The farmer thanked the prince, took the thirty-six fat pigs and gave them back to the farmers.

The white falcon flew back to the troll holding the egg firmly in his claws.

In the mountain the troll was fast asleep on the princess's lap. The prince came in with the egg in his hand shouting to the troll that he had something for him. The troll jumped up from the princess's lap and turned towards the intruder. Before he could do anything, the prince threw the egg with the troll's heart inside it onto the forehead of the troll. The egg broke and killed the troll immediately. The princess stood up and gave her beloved husband a kiss. They found the exit to the cave and found themselves back at the castle. There was much joy and celebration when the prince and the princess entered the castle.

And so it was that the shoemaker's son after the death of the old king became the King of Spain and his beloved queen and he often walked around in their kingdom enjoying the sun.

22

THREE MERRY WIVES

I can recognise myself in these fools. Luckily my wife has never put my foolishness to the test.

There were three houses next to each other. In one lived a tailor, in the second a carpenter and in the third house lived a blacksmith. The wives of the three men were very good friends. Often the three women talked about how stupid their men were, but they could never agree upon which of the men was the stupidest.

The three wives went together to church on Sundays, and as they walked on their way to the church they talked of all things good, but it was after church when they came into the local inn and bought one half pint of snaps that the laughter started. It was in those days when a half pint of snaps cost three shillings, one shilling for each of the three merry wives.

One Sunday afternoon when the three women met at the inn the inn-keeper told them that the price of a half pint of snaps was going to cost four shillings starting from next Sunday. That was bad news for the three women, because four shillings divided to three doesn't work. They decided it would be easier for two of them to pay two shillings and the other get snaps for free. But which one of them would that be?

As they walked home they talked about it and agreed that a good bet would solve the issue of who should pay and who shouldn't. The woman with the stupidest husband would be the winner and that should be settled next Sunday. The one that had made the biggest fool of her husband would have snaps for free for a whole year.

Next day the tailor's wife told her husband that she was going to card wool together with a large group of young women. She said, 'There is so much to do before the evening. It is a pity we don't have our guard dog any more because tonight we will have all the young men from the village here trying to disturb the young girls so no work will be done. Oh, I wish we had a decent dog so he could chase the young boys away from our house.'

'Yes,' said her husband, 'that would have been very good.'

'Here my little man,' said the woman. 'You should be that dog and frighten all the young men away with your barking.'

The tailor didn't think he could do it even if he wanted to do everything possible to please his wife.

'No, you will be good,' she said, and in the evening she gave him a coat with woollen fur and placed a large metal chain around his neck and he started barking and howling at anyone that came near him. And he did such a good job she gave him a biscuit. The three wives had a good laugh about that.

Next day, when the carpenter had been out to work and came home, his wife was waiting for him with his dinner. When he stepped inside, his wife looked at him in horror and said, 'My you look sick. You look like something is terribly wrong with you.'

The carpenter didn't feel bad at all, he was just hungry and said it was just a question of him getting something to eat then he would be fine. He sat down and started eating his dinner. His wife sat opposite her husband looking at him with great concern.

'It is just getting worse and worse, now you are paler than I ever had seen. And look how you are trembling. You are very sick, my dear, it is very serious this sickness of yours.'

The carpenter started feeling a little sick. Maybe it was true what his wife said to him, it nearly always was.

She said, 'It is time for you to go to bed, maybe that will cure it, but I am afraid it will not.'

She made him go to bed, found all the blankets and duvets in the house and put them around him, gave him elderberry tea and a hot water bottle and the carpenter got more and more feverish and sick.

'You will never make it,' his wife said, 'I am afraid I am going to lose you.'

'Do you really think so?' he said, 'I am feeling terribly ill now, so maybe you are right.'

Suddenly she frowned and said, 'Now we are going to part. It is death coming to take you. Let me close your eyes.'

And she closed the carpenter's eyes and he believed everything she told him, so he was sure he was dead. He just lay there with closed eyes and folded hands.

So she called on her two friends to help lay him down in one of his own coffins. She made holes in it for him, so he could breathe, and made it comfortable with blankets and a pillow. Once inside the coffin she covered him with a warm blanket and instead of flowers she gave him a little bottle of snaps. They closed the coffin and the three women heard him taking one sip of the good liquor, then another and then a third. Soon they heard a gentle snoring sound coming from the coffin. The carpenter was fast asleep, dreaming that he was in heaven.

Soon it became known in the whole village that the carpenter had died and that he was going to be buried the next day. The wife of the blacksmith went to her drunk husband, who was fast asleep in their bed. She pulled off his shirt and covered him in black soot from head to foot. She let him sleep all morning until she spotted the funeral procession for the dead carpenter moving towards the church on top of the hill. Then she ran into her husband and woke him and said, 'What are you doing, you drunk husband, you are late for the funeral procession!'

'What funeral procession?'

The blacksmith was hardly awake and very confused. His wife said, 'It is our neighbour, the carpenter, he died last night while you were at the inn drinking. He is going to be buried today and they are already halfway to the church. Hurry now and join the procession before it is too late.'

'I need my Sunday clothes then,' he said.

'Nonsense,' she said, 'can't you see that you are already wearing them?'

The blacksmith looked down on his body and could see that he was more black than he normally was and if his wife told him, then it had to be so.

She said, 'Here is your hat, now off you go!'

He put the hat on his head and hurried out of the door. The funeral procession was close to the church when the blacksmith, naked as the day he was born and covered in soot, cried out to them, 'Wait for me, Let me have him.'

The funeral procession turned around and thought it was the Devil himself coming for the carpenter and they dropped the coffin and ran away. When the coffin hit the ground, the lid of the coffin bounced off and the carpenter woke up, sat up and looked around. He knew he was dead and that he was attending his own funeral, but when he saw the blacksmith, he said in a quiet low voice, 'Dear neighbour, it is good that I am already dead, because if I wasn't, I would have laughed myself to death the way you are dressed for a funeral procession.'

The carpenter's wife won one year of free snaps because the two others agreed that she had best fooled her husband.

23

PEDER OXE

A degn was a central figure in the Danish villages. He helped the priest with practical things concerning the sermon and he taught the children to read and write. When you hear that a degn is part of a story in Danish you know that there is a trick to be played.

Once there was a farmer and his wife. They were getting older every day like we all are. They had never been blessed with a child and that was a point of deepest sorrow in their lives.

One day their cow gave birth to a lovely calf with the sweetest brown eyes, a shiny reddish brown coat and the softest voice.

It was the woman's duty to take care of the calf and when she did she started talking to the little animal.

'We are doing well here on the farm,' she said with a smile. 'You know, your mother is one of five cows giving us enough milk to sell a little and the sheep bring us wool and all our chickens give us eggs and the fields are full of ...'

She stopped her talking and looked at the calf. It stood there so patiently and she saw a sadness in its eyes. It was as if it knew that behind all the praising of her animals the woman was deeply sad because she was without a child.

'You know?' she asked the little calf. And the calf nodded to answer its 'yes' to the woman. It gave a little sound, it wasn't a normal calf 'mooh'. No, it was more a 'Ja!', the Danish word for yes. The calf stepped forward and laid its head in the lap of the woman, who gently stroked it.

And from that moment on she talked to the calf more and more every day. At first her husband was very suspicious, but when he joined them in the barn he saw that she was right. The calf really did answer all of her questions and gave her 'Ja' or 'Nej' (the Danish word for 'no') in the right places.

So they went down to the calf whenever they could find a little break in what they were doing and more and more they became convinced that the calf was the cleverest animal that ever was born.

'We should name it,' said the woman.

'We should,' said the farmer. 'What would you have called our son, if we ever had one?'

'Peder,' said the wife.

'Me too,' said the farmer, and talking to the calf, he said, 'Your name is Peder.'

And the calf said 'Ja' and from that day on they called his name and he came running.

One Sunday at church they told the degn about their calf and how clever he was that maybe he should go to school. The degn looked at the two and saw that they were not mad and they clearly believed that the calf could become something special.

'His name is Peder,' the farmer's wife said, 'and he is going to be a student one day.'

'I can follow you to your farm and see for myself,' the degn said.

And so he followed the farmers back to their farm. And he told them that he had to talk to the calf alone to see if they were right, and if he was as clever as they said. So he went to the calf and stayed there for a good time talking to it. The calf gave its 'moohs' back to the degn once in a while.

When he came out, he said, 'It is indeed a very special calf you have there, you are truly blessed. I taught your calf a little bit of the alphabet and we did some beginners' maths, and after a few exercises Peder found his way into the deep wisdom of counting and adding.'

'I knew it,' said the woman. 'He is just so clever.'

'I could bring him to the school in the big town and he can start school tomorrow,' said the degn. 'It will cost a little money for you to cover the expenses of his board and tuition.'

The farmer and his wife said that it was no problem as long as Peder was given all the opportunities of an education.

So the farmer went in and came back with a little bag of money.

'Just tell us when you need more,' the farmer said.

The woman kissed the calf goodbye and told it that everything was going to be so good. That the calf was going to have that education she and her husband never got.

The following Saturday the degn sat home in his house having his dinner, when there was a knock on the door. When the housemaid opened the door, it was the farmer and his wife standing outside. As they entered, the degn ate the last bite of the veal on his plate, wiped his face and gently asked the farmers what they wanted.

'To hear news about Peder,' said the woman.

'Yes, Peder, he is doing so well,' said the degn. 'You were right, he is clever. And especially maths. It is his favourite topic. Already after a week he is catching up with the other boys in his class. And he is allowed to sleep with the other boys in the dormitory. He is very happy and told me to say thank you for everything you are doing for him.'

'It is really the least we could do for our Peder,' said the woman, and the farmer handed over a bag of money to the degn, who thanked the couple and promised to tell them whenever there was any news.

Every week the degn went to the farmers and told them about all the progress their calf had made in school.

Years passed by and the degn made poems, wrote theses about geography and in particular showed them complicated maths that their son had supposedly solved. And one day he told them that Peder the calf had somehow, perhaps due to his education, transformed into a young man and that the young man was going to study accounting. And that week the farmer gave the degn the little bag of money with a big smile.

'I knew it,' said his wife. 'He is going to look after us, when we are getting too old to handle the farm.'

The farmer and his wife were really getting very old and they talked to the degn about handing over the farm to their son. The degn told them that it was no good.

'Your son isn't interested in farming, he wants to have his own shop, a butcher's shop, and last time we spoke he had found one he was interested in,' said the degn.

The old couple smiled as they imagined their son in a nice clean butcher's shop.

'Can we go and see him?' the old woman said.

'I will arrange that,' said the degn.

And so he went into the big town and went into a butcher shop with a big sign saying 'Peder Oxe, a butcher to be trusted!'

He asked the butcher if there was a place where they could talk. Peder showed the degn into his office.

'What would you say, if I could give you a mother and a father?' said the degn.

And so the degn told Peder the whole story and there were many 'oohs' and 'aahs'. 'It is strange that you should ask me,' said

Peder, 'I am an orphan, and I never knew my parents. I will meet these people and be their son if they accept me.' Though Peder understood that in the eyes of the old couple he was once a calf.

'I think they will,' said the degn.

The farmers had never been to the big town before and the degn had to help them as they crossed the busy streets. When they saw the butcher's shop with the name Peder Oxe written in big letters, they swelled with pride. 'It is even bigger than I imagined,' said the woman.

'Now go in and talk to Peder, he is expecting you,' said the degn.

They turned to the degn and thanked him so much for everything. He said it was nothing and helped them cross the street. He waved as he said his final goodbye.

The two farmers opened the glass door to the shop and stepped inside. It was the smell that made him stop, it was the sight of Peder that made her stop. So they stood there just inside the shop and stared at it all. The butcher's shop was really impressive. Everywhere they looked there was meat from cows, sheep, pigs and all kinds of birds.

Behind the counter a man was busy cutting some veal into steaks. They looked at his neck and saw how much it looked like a bull's neck. The farmers looked at each other and smiled. A woman asked if she could get something for them. The farmer said, 'No thank you, we are here to talk to our son.'

At that moment the butcher stopped his chopping. The bull's neck stood up still with his back to the farmers and slowly he turned around. The farmers immediately recognised the gentle brown eyes of the calf and knew that this was in fact their clever son. Peder Oxe saw the two lovely old people and saw the love in their eyes, and he couldn't help it. His eyes filled with tears, he looked at the farmer and said 'Far!' and the old farmer cried with his son. And then he turned to the old woman and said 'Mor!', and the old woman nodded, that was what she was. Peder's mor!

THE RIVER MAN

The Danish name for this story is Åmanden. So if you know how to pronounce å, just replace the word river in the story with the word å.

The highest hill in Denmark is 173 metres high and therefore our rivers are small and the speed of the water is moderate. We call a small river like that an å.

In a super flat landscape like the landscape of Lolland the å'er were slow and dull and very small. One of these å'er was Ryde å.

Ryde å in the days of our story started just outside Ryde, a small village, then it ran through the flat landscape until it found the sea not far from *Øllingesøgård*. It must have been a larger and more vital å than it is today, when it is just a small ditch with a little water and not flowing at all.

Niels Paulsen was a young man, no family yet. He had recently graduated from the Royal Agricultural School in Copenhagen and was on his way to his first assignment as a farm steward on the Øllingesøgård estate. The estate was located on the dark, flat island called Lolland as far from civilisation as you can go in Denmark. The lord of the estate wanted to modernise his farm and Niels knew he was perfect for the job.

On his way down south he looked out on the flat landscape of Zealand. More and more poverty and hopelessness was revealed as the coach journeyed further and further away from Copenhagen. After Køge he fell asleep and didn't wake up until the coachman called out, 'We are in Græshave. You told me that it is where you want to get off.'

Niels tumbled down from the coach, the coachman gave him his luggage and waited for a tip, though that never came. Niels stood in the late afternoon sun and looked at the smallest town he had ever been in. A church, a grocers shop, a shoemaker, a blacksmith, a barn and four houses, that was it.

'Welcome, hr. Paulsen,' said an old man standing waiting for Niels. 'I hope you had a good journey down here.' It was an old man with kind eyes and weathered skin.

'Yes,' said Niels. 'It was fine.'

'I am the old farm steward and I am going to resign as soon as you can take over all my duties,' said the old man as he took Niels's luggage to a coach standing on the other side of the little high street.

A young woman, very young indeed, passed by and stared at the stranger.

'Hello, Lisbed,' said the old man to the young woman. 'This is the new steward on Øllingesøgård.'

She smiled and nodded at the stranger. Lisbed went into the grocers shop and locked the door. Niels could see that she very quickly turned around inside the store and peered through the curtains.

The old man drove Niels up to Øllingesøgård, where he was housed in one of the buildings a little away from the main house.

Next day he was shown around by the old farm steward. Niels made a long list of all the things they needed to invest in right away. And the old man made sure that Niels saw every part of the estate. The last thing the old steward showed Niels was the ford, which they crossed to the fields furthest away from the farmhouse. It was located just where the River Ryde approached the sea a few miles to the west. The Ryde twisted its way through the landscape and just on this spot it was shallow enough to pass through the water on foot or with coaches.

'This ford over the River Ryde is where the River Man reigns. When we cross it, we must make an offering to the River Man,' said the old steward. 'If we have a load of potatoes, we give him a sack, if we cross with a basket of eggs, we give him twelve, or some meat or whatever we bring across the River Man's ford. In that way we are safe, the River Man will never harm anyone who shows him kindness.'

When Niels heard of the River Man, a spirit of some kind living in the water, he could hardly hold back his laughter. He didn't say anything to the old man, but in his mind he started thinking how he could use this strange superstition to benefit himself.

And so a new era on the farm began. Niels introduced new machines and new farming methods and it was all very confusing for the farm workers. But Niels assured them that he would always give the River Man what he needed, and when they saw Niels leaving his offerings at the ford the farm workers knew they could always pass safely through the water. The truth was that Niels was filling sacks with potato peelings instead of potatoes or old newspapers instead of rye, wheat or barley, then leaving them in the ford for the River Man. He then took the sacks of real goods down to the grocery shop and sold them. Niels's purse was filling up at great speed.

Lisbed, the daughter of the grocer, watched Niels as he made these shady deals with her father. She knew he was lying to the farm workers and cheating the lord of the estate, but she still was charmed by the young man. There were not a lot of young men around, so when he invited her out for walks in the moonlight and started giving her gifts from the town, she couldn't resist his attention.

Niels thought that Lisbed was rather primitive compared with the countesses and rich ladies of Copenhagen, but he had good fun taking these walks. And when it was cold outside, he invited her into his house to get warm.

After a while Lisbed realised she was pregnant. She told her mother, who told her husband, the grocer.

They came into the kitchen where Lisbed was sitting by the table, crying.

'Well then, you must marry him right away,' said the grocer. 'You are a disgrace to your mother and I.'

'He will not marry me,' said Lisbed sobbing. 'He wants to marry some rich girl in Copenhagen. And he said that he wasn't sure he was the father, because primitive country girls sleep with everyone!'

When the grocer heard this, he threw her out of the house into the winter darkness.

Lisbed sobbed as she walked out of the village towards the ford. It was one of the first days with no frost, so the melting snow had filled the river. When she came to the ford the water was high. She stood on the stone next to the ford and said goodbye to the world, closed her eyes and jumped into the gushing waters. But instead of being swept out to sea she landed on the sandy island in the middle of the River Man's ford and to her surprise she was alive and completely dry. The River Man had refused to accept her as an offering and she knew what he was asking of her. She should live and give birth to the child. She sobbed and cried out, 'But how can I do that? I do not have a home!'

The old shoemaker and his wife were passing that evening and heard her cries. They called out and asked if they could help her. They offered a place to stay in their house and the old shoemaker began to wade into the water. In that moment the River Man's ford became completely dry and the old man could easily walk out to the girl. He gave her his coat and helped her onto the stone on the river-bank, where his wife was waiting. When they left the ford the river roared with the waters that had been held back by the River Man.

Lisbed was given a nice warm bed in the kitchen of the shoemak-ers and when she laid her head on the pillow she silently thanked the River Man for saving her life and giving her a new home.

Niels was beginning to feel the pressure. The lord of the Øllingesøgård estate was angry. He had found out Niels had been stealing from him. And the grocer was furious too. Niels had got his only daughter pregnant and had abandoned her. And one Saturday afternoon Niels looked out of his window and saw that the lord of the Øllingesøgård estate was striding towards his house. Niels looked in the other direction and saw the angry grocer with a walking stick in his hand making his way along the drive. Niels, feeling the threat from both men, decided to run away. Outside his house stood a gig with a horse ready to drive him away from the danger. He grabbed his purse stuffed with money, put a few things in a bag, then ran out and jumped in the gig and with the crack of a whip he was gone.

Niels was speeding toward the ford of the river and he knew once he crossed the ford he would find himself on the road to Nakskov and from there he could get himself to Copenhagen.

But when he entered the ford an incredible force gathered a rising spiral of water beneath Niels, the gig and the horse, lift-ing them ten feet above the water level. It spun them around and around, faster and faster and then flung them out to sea.

The lord of Øllingesøgård and the grocer ran down to the ford looking for Niels. By the time they got there the water was calm. They looked towards the sea and on the beach stood a gig and a horse, shaken but in good condition. Niels was nowhere to be seen.

Soon after this event a young shoemaker came to work in the shoemaker's workshop. The old shoemaker wanted to retire and as he did not have a son, he had made an advertisement in the shoemaker's magazine. The young shoemaker came from the island of Funen. His name was Jakob and when he met Lisbed, there were stars in their eyes.

It didn't worry him one bit that Lisbed carried a child. 'I will make this child my own and there will be many more,' he said with a smile. They were married on a cold March day and when the couple walked down to the ford and left an offering for the River Man they heard a whisper, 'Come here at Easter and there will be money for you!'

So when Easter came in early April, Lisbed and Jakob went down to the ford and searched for the promised money. There was a lot of water in the ford that day and they couldn't see anything that looked like money in the water or on the stones. Suddenly Jakob jumped from the stone on the bank into the middle of the water. Lisbed thought that he had gone mad and she remembered how she had tried to drown herself and that the ford had gone totally dry the moment she had entered the water. It did not happen here. Rather the contrary. Jakob was lifted up and like a boat, he sailed on the water out towards the ocean and he was gone. Lisbed thought that she had lost him. But then suddenly she saw him, waving with something in his hand as he walked back to Lisbed. She smiled with relief and as he came close she saw he was holding a purse full of money.

They were thrilled and started dreaming about how they would spend it on the house and the workshop. But when they looked into the purse and saw the name Niels, they agreed to let the owner of Øllingesøgård decide what to do with all that money. The lord heard the story and told Jakob how he saw Niels being taken away by the River Man. And then he said, 'I think the River Man intended this money for you, Lisbed and the little baby.'

Jakob thanked the owner and insisted that some of the money should be given to the staff of Øllingesøgård as a gift from the River Man, so they always should remember to honour and worship him.

24

SKÆVE

The storm surge on the morning of Friday, 13 November 1872 that hit Lolland, Falster and the islands lying south of Funen was a major disaster. The waves were three metres high and flooded most of the islands, leaving behind wrecked houses, dead humans and animals.

This is the story about what was revealed in the afternoon of that cold November day when people were searching in the water left behind by the sea.

Skæve was born in the village of Græshave in the southern part of Lolland not far from the biggest town, Nakskov. His father was a hero in the civil war in 1848 in Schleswig and died tragically in battle, so Skæve's only memory of his father was a Danish flag on the wall with his father's name written in its white cross. His mother was alone raising her son and she struggled to make ends meet. Skæve suffered from extreme hunger as a very little child. He developed rickets and his back had a peculiar bend. His spine bent from the base to the left, then changed direction and went to the right, then up by the breast it suddenly jutted forward.

Everybody just called him Skæve, which means 'skewed', and he was happy with his nickname.

He was a clever and kind boy when he grew up in the little village of Græshave. He was the boldest of the boys and to play with Skæve was considered an honour. You were never bored if you were in the company of Skæve.

Later when he became a young man, the young girls in the village loved to be entertained by him. He wasn't the most handsome man, but he could make them laugh and he wasn't scared of them, which they enjoyed.

The old gardener on the biggest estate in the area, the Øllingesøgård estate, needed an assistant and Skæve talked his way into getting the job. When Skæve then started working on the farm as the old gardener's apprentice, the gardener saw that the young man had green fingers. Skæve could be gentle and kind to a plant that needed attention. It was like the plants talked directly to Skæve. When it was needed, his arms were as strong as any young man the old gardener had worked with. Skæve worked hard on the farm and soon the old gardener no longer needed to do the heavy work. The old gardener was proud to pass on his knowledge to his fine apprentice.

One of the services a gardener on a big estate like the Øllingesøgård estate had to fulfil was holding meetings with the housekeeper on the estate.

The housekeeper was a very important woman. She was in charge of all matters relating to food for the household. She decided how many potatoes were needed for the winter, or if there were extra oats needed that season.

The meetings between the gardener and the housekeeper often involved going out to the fields looking at the crops, counting how many potatoes were left in stock and making sure the wheat to be sowed was in tip-top condition.

Skæve was employed on the estate in the middle of winter and Miss Jensen the housekeeper enjoyed her meetings with him and the old gardener where they planned for the year ahead. In the beginning the old gardener was leading the meetings, but eventually Skæve took over and when it became spring it was only Skæve and Miss Jensen doing all the walking and talking. They enjoyed each other's company and one day Miss Jensen invited Skæve for a walk later that night. And so they started doing these walks regularly, holding hands, and one special full moon evening Skæve gave Miss Jensen a kiss and asked for her real name. When she gave it to Skæve, he just smiled and told her his. That was the engagement settled.

Now the wedding had to be planned.

On an estate like the Øllingesøgård estate there were other workers. One of them was the steward of the barns on the farm, an important person if you asked him. This steward was in charge of the barns and what was in them. He came to Miss Jensen one late afternoon in the beginning of June and said, 'Is it really true that you are going to marry this Skæve? A simple worker with no fortune or security of any kind. You should reconsider and find someone of your own standard and with no handicap.'

Miss Jensen just looked at him coldly and told him that she loved Skæve and it was none of the steward's business who she was going to marry. He left with a grunt.

The wedding took place on a hot, humid, midsummer's day. The dark rainy clouds were gathering in the distance, but not a drop of rain fell and the air was thick with moisture. So when the two lovers gave their loud 'yes' in the little church, everybody was sweating and thinking that rain and thunder would do everyone some good. After the beautiful ceremony in the church there was a little gathering with Skæve's mother, the lord of the Øllingesøgård estate and his wife and a few friends from the farm.

In the evening the couple were given the guesthouse to spend their wedding night. As they were getting ready to go to bed, Skæve told his wife that he would go into the garden to smoke his pipe. Skæve loved a pipe of tobacco just before he went to sleep. He would find a quiet place, light his pipe and think about the day while he was enjoying the taste of the good tobacco. His wife said that it was going to rain soon, so he should come back when it started. She went into the bathroom to make her final preparations for the night.

The moment she entered the bathroom, the heavens opened up and the rain that had been hanging over their heads all day finally poured down over the little guesthouse. She returned to the main room in the guest house wondering why her beloved Skæve hadn't come in from the rain. Then came the first lightning and immediately after that the crashing sound of majestic thunder. Still no sign of her love. She opened the garden door and the rain came rushing in. She called out into the dark and the rain. No answer. Then another bolt of lightning flashed, and in that flash she thought she saw some men in between the trees carrying something.

She shouted, 'Have you seen my love?'

No answer, just the thunder now a little bit away from the farm. She found a coat and ran out of the guesthouse. There were no men in between the trees, she was all by herself in the dark. She ran to Skæve's mother. No Skæve. She ran to the owners of the estate and apologised for getting them out of their beds, but she was really worried that her love was gone. It was as if he had vanished into thin air. She was trembling with fear and cold. So the lord of the estate and his wife took her inside and made sure she had some hot soup, and dried her clothes. The lord told his servants to search for Skæve but after an hour of intense searching they came back empty-handed. Skæve's wife collapsed when she realised that Skæve was gone. It was so hard to believe that her love had abandoned her like that.

A week after the wedding and the disappearance of Skæve the steward of the barns came to the housekeeper.

'I am sorry to hear about your husband's disappearance,' said the steward, 'but that's just how simple people behave. Your husband was too scared to fulfil his matrimonial obligations and ran away when you asked him to stand up like a real man.'

She stared at him with disgust and said, 'My love is ten times more man that you are ever going to be. I will ask you to leave. I have nothing more to talk to you about if it is not about the livestock on the farm.'

'But you will need a husband now your coward of a man is gone,' said the steward.

'Perhaps,' she said, 'but that is my decision alone, not yours. Please leave me now.' So the steward finally left.

She sat down and cried. She thought of Skæve and felt his warm and gentle touch as his spirit embraced her.

Soon the belly of Skæve's wife grew and it became obvious that Skæve hadn't been too scared of fulfilling his matrimonial duties on the wedding night as proposed by the steward. Skæve had already done his duty and his wife was now pregnant with their child.

She gave birth to a lovely sound boy at the end of winter just as the snowdrops were beginning to grow. She looked at the baby boy, felt his straight spine and smiled.

The little boy grew up on the estate showered in the love of his mother and everybody else who worked there, except for the steward of the barns. He never spoke to the boy.

When the boy was ten years old, a disaster hit Lolland. In the morning of Friday, 13 November 1872, the wind changed from north-west to a direct wind from the east. It was a cold harsh wind full of rain and snow.

The islanders woke that stormy winter morning and felt the wind blasting across the land. As they got ready to go to work, to school, the waves crashed over the dykes and the flood swept away everything in its path.

The water in the Baltic Sea washed back into the inner fjords of southern Denmark with devastating force. The tsunami was about three metres high and left a deadly trail destroying houses, and drowning animals and humans in the salty water.

When the terrible storm finally stopped, the people from the farm began searching the boggy fields of Øllingesøgård to find their animals or any missing people. They came to some of the forests a short way from the farm. And there they saw a dead hand sticking out from the ground. It couldn't be one of the victims from the flood the same day – this hand appeared to be many years old. When they dug out the naturally mummified body, it turned out to be the remains of a beheaded man. They searched and searched, but couldn't find the head anywhere. The skeleton had a strange-looking spine that bent from the base to the left, then changed direction and went to the right, then up by the breast it suddenly jutted forward. There was no doubt in anyone's mind. They had found the beheaded remains of Skæve.

When the housekeeper was told that her beloved Skæve was found dead in the soil in the forest not far from Øllingesøgård she was in one way relieved. Her one love in her life had not just left her, somebody had killed him and buried him in the ground.

They gave Skæve a funeral and his wife and son were able to say their farewells.

In the evening after the burial it started raining heavily again. A young couple came home from Nakskov and when they passed the graveyard, the young woman screamed as she saw Skæve's coffin rising up from his grave. Was it the water or was it Skæve looking for his head? Well, the priest decided that the coffin should be kept in the church until the ground dried out towards spring.

That winter was hard on every soul in Lolland. Every sack of grain or potatoes in every store room of the farm was needed to feed the people. When the farm workers came to the last of the store rooms it was empty except for two sacks hidden in a dark corner. Inside one they found a broken pipe and a blood-stained axe and in the other they found a skull with a big hole in the front.

A search for the steward was carried out and they found him in one of the barns. He had hanged himself from the ceiling.

Skæve's head was placed in his coffin and that spring they buried him again. This time he stayed in his grave, happy to be united with his head.

26

GÖRAN FROM SWEDEN

Nakskov is not New York.

Göran was a young quiet man from Dalarna in Sweden. He had a dream and the land of dreams was not in Sweden at the time of our story. More than half of the young men he knew had left the village to go to America and Göran was soon going to be one more.

Göran looked around in the village and he saw empty houses belonging to the families who had now migrated to the land of promise.

'Don't cry,' he said to his mother. 'I will return as soon as I am rich enough to do so.'

In Göran's mind that was only a question of a couple of years and then he would be like Mr Svensson. Mr Svensson had sent a letter to the village with photographs showing his new house, his lovely new wife, his children and a new brown hat with a brim broader than anyone ever had seen a brim in all of Dalarna, maybe in all of Sweden.

Göran came to Stockholm and found the boat that would take him to the land of the Statue of Liberty. He had just enough money to buy himself a ticket on the open deck. So he found himself a place on the open deck together with families, young men like himself and a few young women travelling solo to the land of promise. He rolled a blanket out as a bed and sat down on the deck overloaded with impressions. As the time for departure came closer the deck became packed with people.

As soon as the boat left Stockholm and came into the Baltic Sea, the waves made the ship roll from side to side and people on the open deck had a hard time walking. Göran felt seasick. He couldn't help it, the sky whirled around over his head and he tumbled forward and held on to the railing He hung there green and pale and he felt like he was dying.

They passed Gotland, Öland and turned towards west for the first time still with Göran hanging over the railing dying. He was sure he would never make it to America. They passed Bornholm and the crew were now seriously concerned about this man looking so miserable and vomiting the whole day and night.

As the morning came, Göran was more or less unconscious. So they decided to bring him to the next town they passed. The big ship waited as some of the sailors lowered Göran down into one of the lifeboats, where he again just hung over the side. The sailors handed the half-dead body of Göran over to the authorities and continued their journey to America.

Göran found himself on the ground and he could breathe for the first time since he had felt the sea shake his world. He sat up and looked around and the first thing he noticed was the size of a load of sugar beet.

'Wow,' he thought, 'everything is bigger here in America.'

Then he stumbled to his feet and looked towards the town where the impressive sugar factory filled the sky with an enormous chimney and again he was impressed with the size of it.

He was a little surprised by the size of the tiny harbour office with the uniformed personnel. He thought that there would be a giant hall with lots of people on an island where immigrants were welcomed to America.

He stepped into the harbour office, still a little dizzy, and said, 'I ár Göran from Sweden, you know! America ár nice.' Göran pointed at himself and said, 'New York, New York, Statue af Liberty, me immigrate!'

The man behind a counter said mildly in Danish, 'Ja, det kan såmænd godt være, men det her er ikke New York, du er i Nakskov på Lolland og du behøver ikke at snakke engelsk, jeg forstår svensk, min mor var fra Bornholm.' ('Well, it may be true, but this is not New York, this is Nakskov on Lolland and you do not need to speak English, my mother was from Bornholm.')

So it was that Göran landed in Nakskov and found his way out of town to the little village of Græshave, where he lived the rest of his life and never once wished for another attempt to sail on one of those big boats full of Swedish immigrants that passed by on their way to America.

THE POLISH
BEET PICKER —
GÖRAN PART 2

The flat countryside of Lolland was full of sugar factories and every year around Oktober, Lolland saw hundreds of Polish, mostly women, that came over to work in the sugar beet fields.

Göran rented a little house not far from the big farm Øllingesøgård. From time to time there would be some work for him on the farm and other times it was more quiet and they didn't need his services. It fitted Göran perfectly. He liked to be not too involved in the daily life on the farm, and on the other hand it was good money when they did find a use for his skills.

Especially at the time of the weeding and later the harvest of the sugar beet, Göran found himself on the big farm nearly every day.

To clean the sugar beet and later harvest them, a number of Polish women were employed. They worked hard, they never complained and they were happy even though they were paid nearly no money for their services. So they were popular among the farm owners in Lolland and also at Øllingesøgård. Göran noticed the young women but he was much too shy to speak to them and the language was a problem. He spoke Swedish perfectly or he spoke the dialect you spoke when you were from Dalarna in those days. But he had never learned Polish. One of the young

women, with brown hair and a lovely smile, started following
Göran with her eyes when he came down with something to
drink in the summer heat.

One day after work, in the middle of summer, Göran was on
his way home from work when he noticed that the young woman
was standing at the side of the road. Much to his surprise she was
waiting for him. So they walked in the flat landscape and had
conversations like, 'Her er meget fladt!' (Here is very flat!') and
when she didn't understand he would show her with his hands
that the horizon was the same height from right to left. It was
a fantastic walk and it wasn't the last. Soon they started picking
up a few words. 'Spac' was 'sleep', 'burak cukrowy' was 'sugar
beet' and 'owsianka' was 'porridge'. She learned how to count in
Swedish. The number seven, 'shju', always made her laugh.

Göran had a day off from work at Øllingesøgård and went into
Nakskov, the biggest town in Lolland. It was a little bit bigger
than a village at the time of the story, but it had a shop selling
women's clothes and part of that shop was devoted to women's
underwear. He had five kroner with him and he wanted to buy
some pink bloomers he had seen in the shop windows last time
he was in Nakskov. He entered the shop and felt nearly as bad as
he had felt on his way to America. He could hardly breathe and
he was just standing inside the shop not asking for help, doing
nothing, a statue from Sweden in a women's clothes shop somewhere in Denmark. When one of the staff in the shop asked him
if there was anything they could do for him, he mumbled something totally incomprehensible for any Dane and left the shop.

Outside he was quivering with shame. Why didn't he have
the courage to ask for a pair of pink bloomers for his maybe
soon-to-be girlfriend? He ran through town and found himself on some of the smaller roads of Nakskov. There were fine
houses with very neat gardens and hedges, many hedges. As he
was walking around peeking into people's gardens, he stopped,
paralysed. On a clothesline in one of the gardens hung a pair of

pink bloomers exactly the same as he had seen in the shop. There was nobody to be seen, so Göran quietly slipped into the garden, took the pink bloomers off the clothes line and put them in his pocket. In the place of the bloomers he hung a five kroner note.

When the Polish woman received his gift and saw what it was, she blushed. Next time she met him, she had learned two new Swedish words, 'tack' and 'underkläder' ('thanks' and underwear'). Göran blushed and they held hands.

When the last sugar beet had been harvested, it was time for the Polish women to go home. The night before the departure, Göran's Polish friend was nowhere to be seen. He asked her best friends and none of them knew where she was.

And on the day of their departure, Göran stood by the gate of Øllingesøgård and hoped to get a glimpse of the young woman he had become so fond of. She was nowhere to be seen. Had she just hidden herself from him? Something had happened and Göran just couldn't understand what it was.

The Polish women left in November and came back around May for the first weeding of the sugar beets. Göran had gone all the way to Rødby so he could stand by the jetty when the women arrived from Poland and then he could drive with them up to the farm. When the Polish women came down the stairs from the ferry and stood on the pier, Göran's beloved was nowhere to be seen. And they were all silent. Normally the Polish women were famous for all their chattering and their laughs. Göran saw her best friend and went to her. She stood still, crying softly. Göran asked her with gestures where his friend was. One of the young women knew a little Danish and she came over.

'She is dead,' she said. 'She killed herself. On the way over to Lolland she jumped into the sea and drowned.'

'She was pregnant,' said the young woman, 'and we think that she was too embarrassed to show you. She liked you, you know. Just liked you.'

'But how she could be pregnant, we were never together like that,' said Göran.

'No, but we think that the foreman at the sugar production team had his will by force,' the young woman said.

Göran closed his eyes, he could hardly breathe. Then came the tears, like a river of sadness, like a flood of regrets, like a tsunami of hate against that man. He had taken the best thing Göran had ever had.

Her best friend gave him a scarf that he recognised. A scarf that she had worn when they had had their walks. The young woman said, 'Take this scarf as a memory!'

Göran watched the bus with the Polish sugarbeet women drive away from the ferry. His idea that he could drive with them was gone. It fitted him well to walk the long distance from Rødby to Græshave. When it started to rain, it felt better. His tears mixed with the rain and when he came home to the little cottage, he was soaking wet. The scarf was dry; somehow he had managed to keep it away from the rain and his tears.

It was the last time Göran cried. He lived long in Græshave and became known as the Swede. And in a little brown box he kept her scarf. Every evening he held it in his hands. Göran never got married.

28

THE SHOEMAKER
AT WAR

1864 was an iconic year for Denmark. We went into a war to overcome an enemy. It was a disaster. We lost nearly half of Jutland to the Germans in the south.

Just before lunch, as part of his daily routine, Jakob stepped out of his shoemaker workshop in Græshave, Lolland, and took a good look at the high street. The air was alive with the bustle of late March, with everyone and everything getting ready to open up for the springtime.

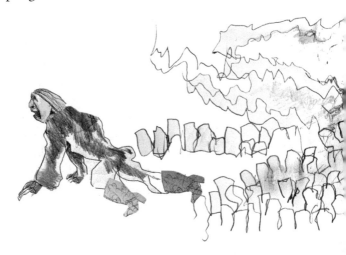

A stranger came walking down the high street and walked straight up to Jakob and said, 'Your country needs you to be a soldier, the Prussians will invade us if we don't mobilise every man.'

'But I am not a soldier,' said Jakob, 'I make and repair shoes. I know nothing about weapons and if there is a loud noise, I run and hide.'

'We can force you, you know,' said the stranger. 'The prison will teach you a lesson and after a couple of weeks locked up, you will be ready to fight for your king and country.'

For Jakob the thought of going to prison was even worse than going to war. So he tried to make a deal with the stranger.

'If I go to Dybbøl to be part of your army and fight the Prussians,' said Jakob, 'will you promise me I will never go to the front?'

'Please don't call it "my army", said the stranger, 'because it is just as much yours as mine. It is for every single Dane that we fight, we protect Dannebrog and the king and Denmark. But yes, I will do my best to make sure you never come close to the front line.'

Jakob was given a letter explaining to his superiors that he wasn't to go to the front line. Instead it stated that Jakob would be most useful taking care of the commandos' shoes and boots.

He somehow got himself across Fyn and over to Dybbøl, where the Danish and the Prussian armies were getting ready for the final battle. In the headquarters of the Danish troops everything was chaos. Soldiers were running around trying to find someone that could tell them what to do and great numbers of wounded soldiers were being brought in from the front line.

As Jakob walked around in the Danish headquarters looking for the commander in chief, he passed soldiers dying on stretchers scattered around in the courtyard.

Jakob recognised one of the young men from Lolland and walked over to him.

'Good day, sir,' said Jakob. 'Do you recognise me?'

'I do,' whispered the young man. 'You are the shoemaker from Græshave. What are you doing here?'

'I am trying to find the commander in chief,' said Jakob, 'I have a letter where he will be instructed never to let me come close to the front line.'

'I wish I had such a letter,' said the soldier before a coughing fit overtook his body. After a while he calmed down and continued. 'We Danes don't have a chance out there. The Prussians load their guns so fast that while we are standing trying to fill our useless guns with gunpowder each Prussian soldier has fired three shots and killed or wounded all of us. Dybbøl 1864 is a disaster and if you survive, tell the Danes: never again!'

Jakob held the hand of the soldier until he lost consciousness, then he found a nurse that said there was nothing she could do but hold the men's hands and let them die.

Jakob found the office of the commander in chief. There were two men arguing loudly.

He knocked on the door.

'Come in,' said a deep voice.

Jakob stepped into the office.

'I am from Lolland and I have this letter to show you,' said Jakob.

The commander read the letter, laughed and handed it to another man who was staring at a map on the wall. He had the biggest moustache Jakob ever had seen. A loud laughter rang out from underneath the enormous moustache. He asked Jakob how much he paid for a letter like that. Jakob explained that he had paid nothing for the letter.

'Well, good, it says that you can take care of my boots,' said the commander.

'I can,' said Jakob.

'Well, make sure that every morning my boots shine like something the cat has left behind,' said the commander.

From that moment Jakob took care of the men's wooden shoes, put new soles on some of the junior officers' shoes and became very popular among the men in the headquarters, and of course made sure that the commander's boots were as shiny as could be.

The fighting between the Prussian troops and the Danish soldiers intensified and the front line came closer and closer to the Danish headquarters. One day a Prussian officer was carried into the headquarters. The commander in chief was told that the man was dying. So he came down to interrogate him as fast as he could, but it was too late, the officer was dead.

The Prussian officer had only his right leg; the left leg had been shot off during the battle. The commander in chief saw the boot on the right leg. It was a boot made of the finest light brown leather you can imagine. It was embossed with a pattern so wonderful that it was hard to believe that the pattern was carved into leather. It was extremely delicate and expressive and the commander in chief told the soldiers to take off the boot from the dead officer. When the commander in chief put the dead officer's boot on, he gave a loud 'Jakob!' out into the courtyard, where he knew Jakob was repairing the men's wooden shoes. When Jakob came to the commander in chief he had one boot on the right leg that was new and one on his left that he recognised.

'Jakob,' the commander in chief said, 'what do you say about this, my new boot?'

'I must say, sir, I have never in my life seen better leatherwork. But where is the other?'

'That is the problem, my dear Jakob,' said the commander in chief. 'The other is in no-man's-land. So I want you to take a soldier with you and find the other boot. It is too beautiful and will make a fine memento of these insane weeks.'

'But, sir, you remember my letter,' said Jakob. 'You promised me I would never come close to combat, and now you want me to crawl around in between the lines.'

'Do I hear you right, are you neglecting an order from your commander in chief? Are you aware of the punishment for desertion?' shouted the commander in chief into the ears of poor Jakob.

A soldier rescued Jakob from more shouting and dragged him away from the courtyard. Jakob knew there was nothing he could do.

Once out on the front line Jakob saw the tiredness of the Danish troops and he could feel the weight of their knowledge that it was only a question of time before the Prussians would make the final push forward.

The soldier led Jakob through a hole in a fence and started crawling into no-man's-land. On one side was the Prussian army and on the other was the Danish. Jakob and the soldier were crawling around among the bodies of soldiers and horses, limbs of soldiers, some wounded soldiers, and the sound of Prussians and Danes crying out for help. Jakob was about to give in and just crawl back, out of this nightmare, home to the workshop in Lolland. But then he remembered the insane face of the commander in chief when he shouted and threatened to shoot him if he didn't find the boot of the Prussian officer.

Suddenly a little bit down towards the little river flowing by, Jakob spotted some light brown, delicately carved leather and he knew he had found it. He crawled down to the boot, which was still on the officer's leg that had been shot off at the hips. Jakob heaved and pulled the boot free from the leg. And then he raised himself onto two feet and was about to scream to the soldier that he had found it, when the soldier tackled him down to the ground. The shooting started immediately from the Prussian side and the Danes retaliated. So Jakob and the soldier had to crawl as close to the ground as possible. They found themselves just a short

distance away from the front line, when they finally dared to stand up. Jakob thanked the soldier and said he had saved his life.

'I probably did,' said the soldier, 'but please wash your trousers. I can smell that you had let go. It happens the first time someone shoots at you. It happened to me as well.'

'Did you follow me just to make sure I didn't hurt myself?' said Jakob.

The soldier nodded.

So Jakob took off his pants and washed them in the river.

Back in the headquarters Jakob found the other boot and he gave them a good clean and polish. When he came down into the courtyard, everybody was busying around. The front line couldn't hold back the latest attack and it was just a matter of hours before the Prussians would take over this farm and the rest of the area around it.

Jakob stood there with the boots in his hand and felt lost. The soldier came over and said that he did good out there in the field and that Jakob could be a good soldier if he wanted.

'Thanks,' Jakob said, 'but I do not think this is for me. I prefer my shoemaker workshop home in Lolland.'

A bomb crashed into the field not far from where they were standing. A quick farewell and in no good order, rather just intense chaos, the Danish headquarters was abandoned. Jakob never saw the commander in chief again, so he never got the chance to see the boots of the Prussian officer on him.

The boots didn't fit Jakob, they were too big, so when he walked through Fredericia he went into a shoemaker and was paid more than twenty kroners for the pair, and that was a lot of money for Jakob. He found his way back to Lolland together with a lot of disillusioned soldiers, who found themselves ridiculed by the Danish people. The politicians and the newspapers had told the Danes that it was just a question of hours, maybe days, before the brave Danish soldier Jens would have kicked these Prussians back to where they belonged. Instead the Danes had to swallow this dreadful defeat and it was hard for a lot of people. The soldiers were easy to blame. But Jakob knew that it wasn't the soldiers' fault, rather it was the politicians that should have asked about whether or not the Danish army was equipped to meet a modern army. As Jakob travelled over Fyn and on the ferry to Lolland everybody was talking about the horrible loss at Dybbøl, and they talked about the fact that the Prussians would take all the land up to Kongeåen and everybody agreed that it was a disaster that had hit the Danish nation.

Jakob didn't say anything; there was nothing to be said. He thought of the soldier who had predicted that the year 1864 would stand in the history of Denmark for a defeat so violent that the Danes would avoid war at any cost in the future.

Jakob found his way back to Lolland and he never spoke about his adventures in Dybbøl in public. He told the story of the boots and the crawling around among dead bodies and horses once to his wife many years later. She had just told him that she was pregnant and that she was scared that they didn't have enough money to get through the winter now that she couldn't work so much with her pregnancy and all. Then Jakob told the story about the boot of the Prussian officer. After the story his wife just stared at him.

'Was it really you, Jakob, all by yourself with all that evilness?'

Jakob nodded and went up, found a little box, and gave it to his wife. She opened it and inside was more than twenty kroner, a good sum of money then. His wife stared at the money, then at Jakob.

'This is more than enough,' she said, 'to get us through the hard times.'

'The money was meant just for that,' said Jakob, and he closed his eyes. The images from those horrible April days were burned into his memory, but now it was like they were softened, like they had a tone of forgiveness. Jakob opened his eyes, looked at his wife stroking her round belly and smiled.

GLOSSARY

ø – en ø = an island / øen = the island
å – en å = a tiny river / åen = the tiny river
ting – a gathering to make decisions
degn – a degn was a central figure in the villages. He helped the priest with practical things concerning the sermon and he taught the children to read and write, so they could read the Bible. When you hear that a degn is part of a story in Danish you know that there is a trick to be played.
Jarl – Swedish earl
skæve – skew-whiff
kælling – old woman
mø – virgin/maiden
lodden – hairy
skjold – shield
mor – mother
far – father
snaps – a liqueur that the Danes also call aquavite. Often made from potatoes, it is an essential part of a Danish julefrokost (Christmas lunch).
øl – beer

SOURCES

1. Danmark
Original title: Kong Dan.
Original source: Lejre krøniken
The Danish storytellers gathered together in a festival from 1998 to 2013 in Lejre Research Centre, a wonderful outdoor museum with houses from the Stone Age. I told Bjowulff down by the black lake there. It was great to have the family with us as part of the festival.

I heard the story of King Dan for the first time from one of the volunteers from Lejre Research Centre.

2. King Skjold
Original title: Kong Skjold.
Original source: Lejre krøniken.

3. Tora and Ragnar
Original title: Tale of Ragnar Lodbrog, part of Völsunga Saga.

4. Kraka and Ragnar Lodbrog
Original title: Tale of Ragnar Lodbrog, part of Völsunga Saga.

5. King Lindorm
Original title: King Lindorm.

From Vendsyssel in the northern part of Jutland. Told by Maren Mathisdatter i Fureby, close to Løkken. Written down by adjunkt Niels Levinsen.

From the small collection *Danske Sagn og Æventyr fra folkemunde*, chosen by Axel Olrik, 1997.

I heard this story for the first time from Anna Lundquist, Swedish storyteller. The story was told from Skagen in the north to Skåne in the east of the original Denmark.

6. The Two Friends
Original title: Tre ravne i galgen.
Storyteller: Jens Mathias Kristensen i Fjaltring, Jutland.
Written down by Evald Tang Kristensen.
Here from Vibeke Arndal, *Eventyr fra Jylland*, 1995.

7. The Fat Cat
Original title: Den tykke kat.
From Stævns in Zealand.
Told by Miss Vagtmann.
Written down by the priest C.M. Bugge in Alstrup, close to Aarhus, Jutland.
From the small collection *Danske Sagn og Æventyr fra folkemunde*, chosen by Axel Olrik, 1997.

8. The Sevenstar
Original title: Syvstjernen.
I have it from *Danske Folkeeventyr, i udvalg ved Ejgil Søholm*. Søholm found it in Otto Gelsted, *Danske folkeeventyr*, 1954.

9. The Sledge
Original title: En slædefart.
I have it from *Danske Folkeeventyr, i udvalg ved Ejgil Søholm*. Søholm found it in Jesper Ewald, *Danske folkeeventyr*, 1954.

10. A Father's Heart
Original title: Sønnen der ramte hjertet.
Storyteller: Farmer Niels Hjerrild, Ørnstrup, Jutland.
Written down by Evald Tang Kristensen.
Here from Vibeke Arndal, *Eventyr fra Jylland*, 1995.

11. The Princess who Became a Man
Original title: Prinsessen der blev mand.
Storyteller: Ane Kristine Olesdatter, Horsens, Jutland.
Written down by Evald Tang Kristensen.
Here from Vibeke Arndal, *Eventyr fra Jylland*, 1995.

12. Three Lessons to be Learned
Original title: De tre lærdomme.
Storyteller: Mette Sofie Larsen, Bindslev.
Excerpt from Evald Tang Kristensen, *Fra Mindebo: Jyske Folkeæventyr*, Apple Books.

13. The High Church of Lund
In 2017 Alice Fernbank and I created a performance called Giants about big people and we still perform it around the world. We found this story on a webpage for Domkirkan i Lund.

14. The Danish Captain
Angelstad Church in Småland, Sweden, is old, from around 1100, and it is special in the way that it has no tower. When I came inside I saw it was special for another reason. On the wall was a black shield in memory of a Danish captain who was executed close to the church the second day of Christmas 1570.
Search the Land of Legends, Ljungby, Sweden, for more information.

15. King Christian IV and Jens Longknife
My aunt and her family lived for many years in Mønsted, not far from the chalk mines where Jens Langkniv was supposed to live.

I am remotely related to Jeppe Aakjær, and his book *Jens Langkniv, af Fjends Herreds Krønikebog* has been of great inspiration.

16. Prince Vildering and Miseri Mø
I have it from *Danske Folkeeventyr, i udvalg ved Ejgil Søholm*. Søholm found it in Jesper Ewald, *Danske folkeeventyr*, 1954.

17. The Devil's Coffee Grinder
Storyteller: Potter Erik Larsen, Uglkær, Jutland.
Written down by Evald Tang Kristensen.
Here from Vibeke Arndal, *Eventyr fra Jylland*, 1995.

18. The Devil and the Blacksmith
Storyteller: Schoolboy Anders Gregersen, Sjørslev, Jutland.
Written down by Evald Tang Kristensen.
Here from Vibeke Arndal, *Eventyr fra Jylland*, 1995.

19. The Devil's Best Hunter
Storyteller: Farmer Niels Frederiksen, Herning, Jutland.
Written down by Evald Tang Kristensen.
Here from Vibeke Arndal, *Eventyr fra Jylland*, 1995.

20. The Mermaid that Laughed Three Times
Storyteller: Farmer's wife Inger Olesdatter i Øster Ørum, Jutland.
Written down by Evald Tang Kristensen.
Here from Vibeke Arndal, *Eventyr fra Jylland*, 1995.

21. The Shoemaker's Boy
I have it from *Danske Folkeeventyr, i udvalg ved Ejgil Søholm*. Søholm found it in Axel Olrik, *Danske sagn og eventyr*, 1929.

22. Three Merry Wives

I have it from *Danske Folkeeventyr, i udvalg ved Ejgil Søholm*, 1954.

23. Peder Oxe

This story I heard many years ago from Jens Peter Madsen, a wonderful storyteller from Funen.

You can find it in Svend Grundtvig's book, *Peder Oxe*.

24. The River Man

Written down by Hans Christian Kruse Rasmussen, of Virum, Denmark, who was born in Græshave, Lolland. He remembered them from his childhood, when the stories were told by Axel Paaske, a craftsman from the town.

25. Skæve

Written down by Hans Christian Kruse Rasmussen, from the same source as The River Man.

26. Göran from Sweden

Written down by Hans Christian Kruse Rasmussen, from the same source as The River Man.

27. The Shoemaker at War

Written down by Hans Christian Kruse Rasmussen, from the same source as The River Man.

The stories 'Göran from Sweden' and 'The Shoemaker at War' are in the wrong chronological order, but I couldn't end the book with the sad ending of 'Göran from Sweden'.

ACKNOWLEDGEMENTS

Tak til (thanks to) all of you who crowdfunded to make it possible for Tea Bendix to create the beautiful illustrations for this book. Forever grateful.

Og tak til Sara, Karen, Asger, Madklubben, Blodbøgen i Kongens Have, Bent Lumholt, Lejre Forsøgscenter, now Sagnlandet, Jesper la Cour Andersen, Anders Granström, Christina Claesson og Susie Haxthausen fra Beretter Akademiet, Kasper Seier Schultz, The Golden Fleece Group in Washington D.C., Christian Bloch former Hans Christian Kruse Rasmussen, Donald Smith, the Scottish Storytelling Centre, Lyths Arts Centre, Neil Sutcliffe, Jan Blake, Stork, Hanne Eble, Anna, Tea Bendix og sidst men bestemt ikke mindst, Alice Fernbank.

Og en speciel tak til Nicola og holdet fra The History Press. I er seje.

The destination for history
www.thehistorypress.co.uk